W0008075

LOVE AND BE SILENT

Forgiveness and Defenselessness

KING LEAR

LOVE AND BE SILENT

Forgiveness and Defenselessness

Kᴇɴɴᴇᴛʜ Wᴀᴘɴɪᴄᴋ, Ph.D.

Foundation for A Cᴏᴜʀsᴇ ɪɴ Mɪʀᴀᴄʟᴇs®

Foundation for A Course in Miracles®
41397 Buecking Drive
Temecula, CA 92590
www.facim.org

Copyright 2004 by the
Foundation for A Course in Miracles®

Printed in China

With love for Helen,
who so loved the two men
whose wisdom and love inspired these books.

CONTENTS

INTRODUCTION TO THE SERIES 1

ACKNOWLEDGMENTS 7

****

INTRODUCTION   Specialness and Defenselessness 11

CHAPTER 1   Helen's Poems–I 23
             "The Holiness of Christmas" 23
             "The Ancient Love" 25
             "Conversion" 27

CHAPTER 2   "I Will Be Still an Instant and Go Home" 39

CHAPTER 3   Christmas Passages 61
             The Holy Instant and Holy Relationships.............. 61

CHAPTER 4   Helen's Poems–II 95
             "The Resurrection and the Life".......................... 95

CLOSING MEDITATION
             "The Holy Christ Is Born in Me Today"................. 103

INDEX OF REFERENCES TO A COURSE IN MIRACLES.................................. 105

INTRODUCTION TO THE SERIES

I have long been a lover of Shakespeare, beginning in my high school years and continuing to the present day. I remember as a student taking my little copy of *Hamlet* with me to Central Park in New York City, sitting under a tree by the lake and reading the great soliloquies as I joined in Hamlet's pessimistic if not melancholic view of the world.

My love affair with the Western world's greatest poet and dramatist coincided with my interest in the work and person of Sigmund Freud, which also began in my adolescence. After all, it would be difficult to be interested in human psychology without at the same time being attracted to perhaps the greatest intuitive psychologist of all, an attribution that Freud would no doubt have made, himself a great admirer of the Bard's psychological brilliance in understanding the unconscious dynamics of guilt and projection.

Shakespeare's keen insight into the psyche of his characters has no equal, so much so that one is frequently tempted to speak of Hamlet, Macbeth, Lear, Cleopatra, Prince Hal, and Richard III, to name just a few, as if they were real people, rather than the mere product of a playwright's genius. The great Oxford professor and Shakespearean scholar A. C. Bradley used to pose questions to his students along those lines, such as: What do you think it must have been like for Cordelia to have grown up with Goneril and Regan as sisters? Bradley's point was that even though the sisters in *King Lear* were already fully grown, and their early years never alluded to in the play, their finely-etched portraits allow us to envision them as a real family, with a real history.

For that very reason, Shakespeare's plays have remained popular for over 400 years. His characters speak to all of us. Indeed, they *are* all of us: Lear's vanity and folly, Hamlet's indecision and conflict, Macbeth's ambition and his wife's guilt, and Othello's jealousy. We relate to these motivations and feelings because they are different aspects of the same thought system of special love and special hate we share together. Though every once in a while we find startling reflections of the role of forgiveness, we remember Shakespeare more for his masterful portrayal of a humanity racked by guilt.

From time to time over the years I have made reference to Shakespeare's plays in my workshops and classes on *A Course in*

Miracles. After one of these, which involved Cordelia's personal response to Lear's folly—"Love, and be silent"—I presented a workshop on this theme. This was in December of 2001, and I integrated my presentation of Cordelia's defenseless response to her father's demands of specialness with the Christmas theme of Christ's birth—or, better, rebirth—in us. In September of 2002 I followed the *Lear* workshop with one built around Hamlet's famous *To be, or not to be* soliloquy, discussing *A Course in Miracles'* teachings on death, the core of the ego's thought system. These two Shakespearean tragedies, therefore, served as the jumping-off point for a discussion of some of the more important themes in *A Course in Miracles*, such as specialness, death, and forgiveness.

After the workshop on *Hamlet*, a woman came up to me and asked about my "Shakespeare series." I answered: "What Shakespeare series? These were only two workshops." However, she obviously had information I did not have, for there soon followed workshops on *Macbeth* ("A Tale Told By An Idiot") and *Othello* ("Specialness: Loving Not Wisely But Too Well") to complete the cycle of Shakespeare's four great tragedies. There was also a workshop entitled "The Quality of Mercy," based on Portia's famous speech in *The Merchant of Venice.* In addition, there have been presentations based on Jacques' mono-logue "The Seven Ages of Man" from *As You Like It*, and on *Julius Caesar.* And who knows what after that? The workshops on the quartet of tragedies have given rise to this book, and perhaps other workshops in this series on Shakespeare and *A Course in Miracles* will inspire sub-sequent volumes. For now, however, we turn to the specific subject of this book: Shakespeare's four great tragedies.

When scholars talk about Shakespeare's tragic heroes, they usually do so in terms of a "tragic flaw," an imperfection in the character of the hero that is the driving force of the play's action. This tradition dates back to Aristotle, who discussed the essence of tragedy in his *Poetics.* Of course he did not have Shakespeare to talk about, but he discussed the dramas of Sophocles, Aeschylus, and other tragedians. He was the first to use the term *hamartia*, a Greek word often used to mean "tragic flaw." It is an interesting word because of its wide con-textual field. For instance, when the Old Testament was translated into Greek, *hamartia* was used to mean "sin"; its use then was continued throughout the Bible, including the New Testament. So *hamartia* not only means "tragic flaw," it also means "sin." In archery, it is the word used to describe an archer missing the target or the mark. And, again, it is the Greek word for imperfection in a person's character. Aristotle's use of *hamartia* almost always was associated with the Greek word, *hubris*, which means "pride" or "arrogance." It is the arrogance or pride of the hero that drives him to destruction.

Aristotle's point, which works as well for Shakespeare as it did for the Greeks, is that in tragic dramas, a hero—someone of personal and/ or social stature—is brought to a tragic end as a result of some imperfection or excess in his character. But the excess of character could also be of a positive nature. Thus we can speak of a tragic flaw not only in the great dramatic heroes, King Lear for example, but also in Lear's daughter, Cordelia, who placed an excessive emphasis on truth and goodness in contrast to her sisters, Goneril and Regan, who were almost pure personifications of evil. More often than not, however, the tragic flaw is identified as negative, a pattern followed in most high school classes on Shakespeare, where it generally is defined rather simplistically: the tragic flaw in Hamlet was that he could not make up his mind and act decisively; Lear's flaw was the folly of pride; Othello's, jealousy; and Macbeth's, ambition.

Shakespeare's own version of the tragic flaw appears in a scene in *Hamlet*, when Hamlet is talking about his deceased father:

> *So, oft it chances in particular men,*
> *That, for some vicious mole of nature in them,*
> . . . .
> *Carrying, I say, the stamp of one defect,*
> . . . .
> *Their virtues...*
> . . . .
> *Shall in the general censure take corruption*
> *From that particular fault...*

$$\text{(I,iv,23)}^1$$

It is that defect, Hamlet's "particular fault," that constitutes the tragic flaw or imperfection in the hero.

Thus, again, Shakespeare's great heroes reflect our own flawed minds, born of separation and guilt. Reading of them, moreover, helps

---

1. All Shakespeare quotations are from: *William Shakespeare • The Complete Works •* The Edition of the Shakespeare Head Press, Oxford (New York: Dorset Press, 1988). Line numbers cited refer to the first line quoted.

us connect with our faulty choice, so that we can make a better one. And so, we briefly examine the four plays that comprise the subject matter of these books.

The central theme in *King Lear* is forgiveness, the Holy Spirit's defenseless answer to the ego's specialness. Recall the statement in *A Course in Miracles* that the ego speaks first (T-5.VI.3:5), and the Holy Spirit is the Answer. As recounted in the volume on *King Lear*, Lear acts out of specialness, luring his two eldest daughters—who participate quite happily, it should be added—into the ego's dance. Cordelia, his youngest child, however, refuses to join in, resulting in her father's wrath and punishment. In her perception, however, nothing was done, as exemplified in the repetition of the word "Nothing" when confronted by an irate Lear. Throughout his tirade, throughout the ensuing tragedy up to and including her and her father's death, she is the model of defenselessness and forgiveness.

Cordelia thus exemplifies *A Course in Miracles*' important principle: *not to make the error real.* In other words, she does not give her family's decisions for separation and attack the power to disturb her peace, for she on some level recognizes the dangerous path of the ego's principle of *one or the other*: for one to win, another must lose. Cordelia's silent response of love thus epitomizes the advanced teacher of God, whose gentle patience is almost infinite, knowing the outcome of love is as certain as He is.

It should also be mentioned that the December workshop, originally entitled "A Christmas Message: Love, and Be Silent," was built around the holiday's symbolism, and so the reader will find numerous references to the "Christmas sections" of *A Course in Miracles*, not to mention some of Helen's poems that were written down during the holiday season. These specific references serve as the framework, as does Shakespeare's poetic and dramatic genius, within which the Course's timeless message of forgiveness can be presented.

Hamlet, perhaps the world's most famous play, presents us with no inspiring examples of right-minded thinking, such as we find in *King Lear*. Indeed, forgiveness is the furthest thing from the minds of Shakespeare's characters here, most especially the protagonist, whose infamous inner conflict has made playing his role almost every actor's dream. The pervading theme of death, exemplified in Hamlet's *To be, or not to be* speech, is the focus of the book, specifically the key concept of *A Course in Miracles*: *ideas leave not their source.* Death is the central theme of the ego's thought system of sin, guilt, and punishment, and we are asked in the Course to move past the *form* that death takes in our physical existence to its underlying *content* as a thought. It is that thought that has never left its source in the mind.

Hamlet's melancholic broodings on death provide us with the rich symbolism of the ego's thought system, and leave no doubt about its murderous nature: *one or the other*—one must die so that I might live. In turn, I must die so that some other thing will live. This seemingly endless cycle of death devouring death, masquerading as a cycle of life, gives rise to the pessimism that runs through the play, and Hamlet's character in particular. It is a pessimism that is the only legitimate response to a world in which God is absent. Denying the world's horrific nature—a mistake our Danish hero never makes—can only lead us further away from our single hope: realizing our life is a dream, and at any moment we can choose to awaken from it. Such awakening is not the fate of any of Shakespeare's tragic heroes, but it certainly is the promise of *A Course in Miracles*.

Our next two plays, *Macbeth* and *Othello*, though quite different in mood and action, share a common theme: choosing guilt over innocence, and the terrible consequences that follow. In other words, Macbeth and Othello chose the ego's voice of scarcity and deprivation, and this led to murder and the laws of chaos. Thus, both heroes kill what is most noble and beautiful—the ego's successful seduction of the mind. As we shall see, however, in *Macbeth* this seduction is really internal; while in *Othello*, it is personified in Iago.

Seen from the perspective of *A Course in Miracles*, *Macbeth* presents an incisive portrait of the split mind and the world that arises from guilt. Macbeth's famous speech—*Tomorrow and tomorrow and tomorrow*—is a powerful rendering of the ego and its insane and futile world, represented in the Course in the well-known passage from the text, which begins with the words: "The world is the delusional system of those made mad by guilt" (T-13.in.2:2-10). The characters of Macbeth and Lady Macbeth bring into sharp focus the nature and consequences of the choices offered by the ego, culminating in Macbeth's tortured despair and Lady Macbeth's obsession with her blood-stained hands. The play ultimately is about everyone who carries the burden of guilt and chooses not to listen to the voice of sanity within, knowing the dire consequences of such a choice. This discussion of *Macbeth* focuses on a reconsideration of the protagonist's decisions in the light of the teachings of *A Course in Miracles.* Beginning with the authority problem and the principle of *one or the other*, the discussion moves through the ego thought system to the Holy Spirit's healing perspective of forgiveness, which sees everyone as sharing the same interests and needs.

Othello offers a penetrating if not painful insight into the nature of guilt: its origins in our special relationship with God, and its shadowy expression in our personal life of special relationships. Othello's choice to believe in Iago's lies—the ego's thought system—rather than Desdemona's innocence—the Atonement—is discussed from the perspective of our need to destroy love, and then to experience the horrific consequences of the ensuing guilt. Othello's decision to trust his "friend" and murder his wife on grounds of infidelity is irrevocable; not so, however, our decision for the ego, which can be undone in the instant we choose to trust our true friend and practice his lessons of forgiveness. Thus does Jesus add a "sixth act" to Shakespeare's five-act tragedy, and this discussion of forgiveness provides a suitable conclusion to our discussion of Shakespeare and *A Course in Miracles.*

In summary, *King Lear, Hamlet, Macbeth,* and *Othello,* taken together, present a powerful account of the ego's thought system of guilt and hate. They provide glimpses into its nightmare reality, at the same time their tragic grandeur, reflected in the noble language of some of Shakespeare's finest poetry, leads us beyond life's tragedy to the joy of awakening to the truth.

Before closing this introduction, I should like to say a word or two about Helen Schucman, scribe of *A Course in Miracles,* and the process of writing these books. Helen was a great lover of Shakespeare, and was thus most happily surprised when midway through the scribing of the text the dictation began to slip into iambic pentameter, the meter of Shakespeare's blank verse, with the poetry increasingly becoming a part of the Course itself. I therefore dedicate this book to her, as I know the Course's scribe would be pleased with its theme, as she was with the Shakespearean references scattered throughout her beloved Course. My frequent quoting of Helen's poems reflect her presence throughout the original workshops, as well as in the writing of these books.

Acknowledgments

These books reflect a process of editing and expansion of the original workshops. They have been adapted from the medium of informal lecture to the printed word. Nonetheless, we have attempted to retain the informal nature of the workshops so that the reader may have the experience of participating in a live presentation. The books were all prepared in the same way. After the workshops were transcribed, a preliminary edit was done by Joseph Jesseph, a former staff member of the Foundation and longtime friend, to whom I am very grateful for his wonderful help. Our Director of Publications, Rosemarie LoSasso, then performed a second edit, preparing the way for my final editing and revision. I am especially grateful to Rosemarie, who with great and loving care shepherded this project from the taping of the original workshops to this publication. And to Gloria, whose loving presence in my life remains the ultimate inspiration for my work.

KING LEAR

LOVE AND BE SILENT

Forgiveness and Defenselessness

INTRODUCTION

SPECIALNESS AND DEFENSELESSNESS

The title *Love, and Be Silent* is taken from Shakespeare's mightiest of all tragedies, *King Lear*, specifically the opening of the play when Cordelia, the youngest of Lear's three daughters, says the words: "Love, and be silent." I begin by discussing this scene as a backdrop for the Christmas message, which is actually a message for all days: *Love, and be silent.*

Lear, the aging king of England, is planning for his retirement. He has three daughters and plans to divide his kingdom among them. The largest and best portion will go to the daughter who loves him the most. His two eldest, Goneril and Regan, do not love him at all, and the former speaks first. I am not going to read what she says, but merely point out the effusiveness of her protestations of love for her father. Lear was probably a wise man earlier in his life, but now wisdom has been replaced by folly. He is taken in by the flattery, which almost everyone else knows is insincere. When Goneril finishes her speech, Cordelia, who truly loves her father, says to herself: "*What shall Cordelia do?*" Her answer: "*Love, and be silent*" (I,i,62).

Lear then turns to his second daughter, Regan, and asks her the same question. She responds with even more effusiveness about her filial love, trying to outdo her sister. Lear is once more taken in, and Cordelia again speaks to herself:

> *Then poor Cordelia!*
> *And yet not so; since, I am sure, my love's*
> *More richer than my tongue.*

(I,i,76)

Her love for her father has no words. Moreover, she cannot participate in the charade.

It is now Cordelia's turn, and Lear confronts her, the daughter he loves the most, with whom he had planned to spend the end of his life.

"*Speak,*" he commands.

Her response: "*Nothing, my lord.*"

Lear becomes indignant and snaps back: "*Nothing!*"

And she repeats: "*Nothing.*"

11

Lear will have none of it, and retorts:

Nothing will come of nothing: speak again.

(I,i,86)

Cordelia does speak now, and it is interesting that while she originally thought her response would be to love and be silent, it is clear her meaning was not the silence of words but one of *content*. In other words, she will not participate in the repulsive game of specialness and will be silent to its lure.

Lear gives her still another chance, and his beloved daughter responds:

Unhappy that I am, I cannot heave
My heart into my mouth: I love your majesty
According to my bond; nor more, nor less.

Lear is hardly pleased, and offers her one last opportunity:

How, how, Cordelia! Mend your speech a little,
Lest it may mar your fortunes.

He is threatening her with disinheritance, but the other-worldly Cordelia is hardly interested in earthly rewards or gain. Moreover, she invites her father to a lesson in true love versus the ego's special love:

Good my lord
You have begot me, bred me, loved me: I
Return those duties back as are right fit,
Obey you, love you, and most honor you.
Why have my sisters husbands, if they say
They love you all? Haply, when I shall wed,
That lord whose hand must take my plight shall carry
Half my love with him, half my care and duty:
Sure, I shall never marry like my sisters,
To love my father all.

(I,i,96)

What Cordelia is expressing here is understandable from the perspective of *A Course in Miracles*' teachings on specialness. One of the marks of special love relationships is that we love some people more than others. Moreover, specialness is always exclusive, for it does not embrace all members of the Sonship equally. A principal criterion of a holy relationship is its *inclusivity*, not in *form*, but *content*. Genuine love embraces all people without exception, as distinguished from special love, which selects some people to the exclusion of others and loves certain aspects of certain people to the exclusion of other aspects. Special love, in other words, is never total. It is an expression of sacrifice; the belief in the principle of *one or the other*. Someone has to be sacrificed—if I love you, I cannot love anyone else.

Cordelia is explaining that her two older sisters' claim that they love their father exclusively must mean that they do not love their husbands. Cordelia is saying that her love for her father would not exceed her love for her husband, if and when she marries. Her love for both would be the same. At this point Lear is under the bondage of his specialness needs, demanding that he receive *all* his daughters' love. He thus becomes furious when Cordelia does not offer the specialness he seeks, setting into motion the tragedy in which Lear suffers the dire consequences of his demands for love.

Feeling his daughter has exhausted all her chances, Lear explodes:

> *Let it be so,–thy truth, then, be thy dower:*
> *For, by the sacred radiance of the sun,*
> *The mysteries of Hecate, and the night;*
> *By all the operation of the orbs*
> *From whom we do exist, and cease to be;*
> *Here I disclaim all my paternal care,*
> *Propinquity and property of blood,*
> *And as a stranger to my heart and me*
> *Hold thee, from this, for ever. The barbarous Scythian,*
> *Or he that makes his generation messes*
> *To gorge his appetite, shall to my bosom*
> *Be as well neighbour'd, pitied, and relieved,*
> *As thou my sometime daughter.*

(I,i,108)

Hell hath no fury as specialness scorned.

The lesson of *King Lear* is *simpatico* with the message of *A Course in Miracles*: Love—if it is true love—must be all-inclusive. Needless to say this is extremely difficult. It is almost impossible in this world not to love, or identify with certain people or groups at the expense of others. We see this in war—throughout history and up to the present day. We see it in religions, and in all aspects of our lives. There is always someone or some group—small or large—with which people identify at the expense of another, with only rare exceptions. This belief in sacrifice keeps specialness alive and well.

The origin of specialness is the original special relationship with God, when we, as one Son, became indignant that He would not give us what we wanted. As the text states:

> You who prefer separation [i.e., specialness] to sanity cannot obtain it in your right mind. You were at peace until you asked for special favor. And God did not give it for the request was alien to Him, and you could not ask this of a Father Who truly loved His Son. Therefore you made of Him an unloving father, demanding of Him what only such a father could give. And the peace of God's Son was shattered, for he no longer understood his Father. He feared what he had made, but still more did he fear his real Father, having attacked his own glorious equality with Him (T-13.III.10).

Thus we rejected our Creator and Source, and chose instead the god of specialness. At that point we threw in our lot with the ego, which became our replacement for the special love relationship God could not offer. Identifying with its thought system of individuality and uniqueness, we gladly accepted its gifts of specialness. Despite the fact that the Holy Spirit—the memory of God's Love—came with us into the dream, we continued and still continue to throw away His gift of Love in favor of the ego's gifts, which guarantee the survival of our special identity.

I have at other times drawn a parallel between this scene in *King Lear* and the mythical separation story reflected in *A Course in Miracles*. In the Course's myth, the decision-making part of our minds is confronted with the ego and the Holy Spirit, and, in effect, we go to both parties, asking if they love us and what gift they are offering in exchange for our devotion. The "us" that we want loved is the "us" that is special—an individualized, separated self that sees itself as differentiated from the Self of God. Thus we go to the ego, who in *King Lear* would be represented by the two older sisters, and it tells us how much it loves us—how pleased it is with what we have done by separating from our Creator. Moreover, this ego will reward us by perpetuating our individual existence. As in the story of Lear, the ego says exactly what we want to hear.

Once the separation occurred, we experienced an exhilarating rush with the thought that we were now free. No one could tell us what to do anymore. We could be our own creator, boss, and self. It goes without saying that the ego substantiated these ideas, telling us the wonders of individual existence; what a glorious thing we did by separating from God and establishing our autonomy. Moreover, if we joined with the ego and pledged it our undivided allegiance, it promised we could build our own kingdom: the kingdom of self—all we had to do for this to happen was choose it over the Holy Spirit.

After hearing the ego, the decision-making part of our minds turned to the Holy Spirit (represented in the play by Cordelia), and asked: "What will You do for me?" The Holy Spirit's answer was a quiet "Nothing." So, as did Lear, we furiously demanded: "What do You mean, nothing?" The answer again was "Nothing." Again, with the king, we replied: "Nothing will come of nothing." And then added: "Away with You! I [to cross plays] have found *metal more attractive*" (*Hamlet*, III,ii,114).

Clearly, the Holy Spirit did not give us the answer we wanted: how wonderful we are, how glorious is this individualized, separated, differentiated, and autonomous self. Just as Lear banished Cordelia from his kingdom and conferred his trust, love, and power to his remaining daughters, so did we, the one Son of God, banish the Holy Spirit from our kingdom, conferring our trust, love, and power to the remaining ego.

Lear ends up totally bankrupt, disenfranchised by his eldest daughters and cast out into the heath, where he goes mad midst a raging storm. Lear eventually recognized his mistake, but we do not recognize ours, at least not until the pain of our lives becomes excruciating. Throwing our lot in with the ego, entrusting it rather than the Holy Spirit with our treasure, does indeed bankrupt us. It reinforces the original decision to abandon our treasure as Christ, the one Son of God. In trusting the ego we cast aside the Holy Spirit, Who retains the memory of Christ for us, and we end up with nothing. The pain of that nothingness becomes so acute that we do everything possible to defend against it. To protect ourselves from feeling the enormity of that pain, our primary defense becomes the special relationship.

We chose this individualized, separated self over the one Self of Christ, unified with God, giving rise to the principle of *one or the other*. The thought system of separation and specialness was thus born when we chose the self of the ego, and is continually nourished by the idea of *one or the other.* We thus bankrupt ourselves and go through our lives desperately trying to cover up the pain of our emptiness, believing that we have lost our treasure and now have nothing. This sense of loss leads us to believe the only way we can survive is to take from the outside in order to fill up the gaping hole within. Taking from others becomes the only means at our disposal for fighting against this horrible experience of nothingness. That is the essence of the special relationship: trying to seize from outside what we believe is lacking in ourselves.

We can now see why the special relationship is cannibalistic in nature. *Cannibalism,* incidentally, is not a word found in *A Course in Miracles* (although Jesus used it a couple of times when he was dictating to Helen), but its process is certainly described by the Course— sometimes in excruciating detail—and it follows when our sense of bankruptcy leads us to perceive that someone else has what we lack. Our ego tells us others have what is missing in us because they took it from us, justifying our taking it back. The basis for cannibalism is the idea that someone else has power that I lack and need; someone else has my treasure—a "priceless pearl" that should be mine. As is explained in "The Laws of Chaos" (T-23.II.11), the reason I cannot find my treasure is that my brother hid it in his body. Therefore I have to take it from there, the meaning of cannibalism: I take from someone else what I believe I need and is rightfully mine.

We can see the principle of *one or the other* clearly reflected here. Either you have the treasure or I do, but not both of us; if I lack it, it must be in you. The "you" who must have what I lack is anyone on whom my ego's eyes light, at any given moment in my life. It could be found in a past or present relationship, or one dreamed of in the future. Whatever it is I lack, someone else must have. We all experience that lack as we walk the world of scarcity, otherwise we would not be here. In a sense, we come here looking for something that is missing in our minds. But what is truly missing is the innocence of Christ; the treasure we threw away, just as Lear threw away the innocent love of his daughter, Cordelia. He threw innocence away, so now he believes he is without it and, moreover, does not deserve it. All that remains is the vicious, duplicitous love of his other two daughters. Much later in the play, Lear's trusted friend, the Earl of Kent, observes his king's guilt, the *"burning shame"* that at first does not permit his acceptance of the daughter's love he had betrayed:

16

A sovereign shame so elbows him his own unkindness,
That stript her from his benediction, turn'd her
To foreign casualties, gave her dear rights
To his dog-hearted daughters,–these things sting
His mind so venomously that burning shame
Detains him from Cordelia.

(IV,iii,43)

We have done the very same thing: We threw away the innocence of Christ by banishing the Holy Spirit and setting up a kingdom in our minds to replace His. But ours is bankrupt: a kingdom of lack, in which something vital is missing—the treasure of our innocence. Since we do not believe we have it, we look around the world we made up, and conclude that the reason we do not have it is that, again, someone else has taken it.

The state in which innocence is lacking is equivalent to a state of sin and guilt. Following the principle of *one or the other*, if I have the sin (i.e., have lost my innocence), someone else is without it: sin-less, or innocent. I thus am justified in attempting to retrieve my stolen innocence. Shakespeare provides us with two fine examples of what *A Course in Miracles* calls "the face of innocence," wherein someone or something else is made responsible for our misery and unhappiness. Our first comes from the mouth of Edmund, one of the Bard's more famous villains. He is the bastard son of the Earl of Gloster, one of Lear's staunchest friends. Edmund here bemuses man's attempts to blame his character on the stars, but he concludes by dismissing astrological phenomena as the cause of his own bastardy—pardon the pun!—and refuses to attribute it to anything other than his own nature:

This is the excellent foppery of the world, that, when we are sick in
fortune,–often the surfeit of our own behavior,–we make guilty of
our disasters the sun, the moon, and the stars: as if we were villains
by necessity; fools by heavenly compulsion; knaves, thieves, and
treachers, by spherical predominance; drunkards, liars, and
adulterers, by an enforced obedience of planetary influence; and
all that we are evil in, by a divine thrusting on: an admirable
evasion of whoremaster man, to lay his goatish disposition to the
charge of a star! My father compounded with my mother under the
dragon's tail; and my nativity was under ursa major; *so that it*
follows, I am rough and lecherous.–Tut, I should have been that I

am, had the maidenliest star in the firmament twinkled on my
bastardizing.

(I,ii,121)

The second example is the famous statement of Lear himself:

...I am a man
More sinn'd against than sinning.

(III,ii,59)

The tragedy is not my problem, nor caused by me, but is the effect of
the sins of others.

And so we continually find fault in others, criticizing them by seeing *their* sin or guilt, but not our own. If we can give the guilt and sin
to someone else, which we do through attack—making others responsible for our misery and loss of peace—we believe we have regained
the treasure of our innocence, the "priceless pearl." Thus we spend our
lives desperately looking outside for what will fill up our sense of
emptiness, compensating for the inner lack. However, the sense of lack
has nothing to do with what is actually missing, but with a decision we
made in our minds to choose the ego (sin and guilt), thereby choosing
against the Holy Spirit and throwing our innocence away.

The ego sees to it that our identity is firmly rooted in the body, and
it has us believe that our body is caused by other bodies. Being thus
rooted in the physical world, we are not aware we have a mind. Thus
there is no hope of ever changing the decision that led to our experience of lack. We wind up desperately trying to fill this inner emptiness, but the self we think we are is like a sieve: what we put in goes
right through. In other words, specialness is never enough. It satisfies
for a little while, but empties out because there is nothing substantial
to hold it.

To summarize, our experience of emptiness and lack has nothing to
do with anything actually missing in us, but with a decision we made.
Unless that decision is changed, the experience of lack will remain. We
then become driven by what Freud termed the "repetition compulsion":
the compulsion to repeat the endless and unrewarding search for specialness. As *A Course in Miracles* teaches, we continually seek outside
ourselves to find what we think is missing. We sacrifice others in order
to take from them what we want, and once we get it—through cannibalism—the other lacks it. However, specialness never fills our emptiness, for it continually pours through our sieve-like mind. Our endless

and unrewarding search can never end because the source of the loss is never found. It is as if we had a leaky pipe and could not locate the leak's origin. No matter what we do to patch it, it is never the right place and the leak continues. We keep turning to the ego as our plumber, but of course it never lets us know the real source of the problem, which is in our minds.

One of the ego strategies is to distract us with a lot of noise—what *A Course in Miracles* describes as "raucous shrieks" (W-pI.49.4:3). Our bodies make a lot of noise, and our pursuit of specialness is accompanied by a great deal of fanfare: glee and triumph when we get what we want; agony and anguish when we do not. One way or the other, we are always making noise, fulfilling the ego's purpose of drowning out the Holy Spirit's still, small voice—the biblical phrase denoting the Holy Spirit, used in *A Course in Miracles* as well—as we read in the text:

> What answer that the Holy Spirit gives can reach you, when it is your specialness to which you listen, and which asks and answers? Its tiny answer, soundless in the melody that pours from God to you eternally in loving praise of what you are, is all you listen to. And that vast song of honor and of love for what you are seems silent and unheard before its "mightiness." You strain your ears to hear its soundless voice, and yet the Call of God Himself is soundless to you.
>
> You can defend your specialness, but never will you hear the Voice for God beside it (T-24.II.4:3-5:1).

And that, of course, is the whole idea: *not* to hear God's Voice. Cordelia's response—*"Love, and be silent"*—is reflective of this still, small voice we wish to silence.

In spite of the mad goings on in the world—personal and collective—the Holy Spirit's response is always the same: He loves and is silent. He does not respond to the ego's external screaming, nor does He respond to our demands for specialness. As Jesus explains to us, the Holy Spirit does not take away our special relationships; He transforms them. He is not interested in *form* and does not try to change it. He does not advise about behavior, such as telling you to leave a relationship or stay in it. He does not care what you *do* in a relationship, as long as there is no guilt in your mind. *That* is what He cares about. When the Holy Spirit transforms our special relationships He transforms their *purpose*. The ego's purpose is to continue the "raucous shrieks," our

19

devotion to guilt, which we reinforce in ourselves by desperately trying to project it onto others. In the presence of these mad sounds, a cacophony of guilt, the Holy Spirit does absolutely nothing except quietly remind us through His love for us that we can make another choice, reflective of His purpose of forgiveness.

The ego does not want us to change our purpose; it wants us to change the relationship. That is why we embrace relationships, seeking to get what we think we want; and when that does not work—the leak still is not repaired—we throw them away and find others. As the workbook says: "Another can be found" (W-pI.170.8:7). The ego's Yellow Pages is filled with plumbers—all incompetent. There are always those we can target for our specialness needs. There are always those we can hate: individuals, groups, nations. For instance, if you study history you find that the objects of any particular government's hatred change over time. It does not matter whom we hate as long as there is a specific target suitable for our projection. One year a certain person is a friend, a certain government an ally; the next year the friend and ally become our enemy. In five years it changes back again. Our alliances are always changing, and it does not make any difference because the *content* of hatred is still present in our minds, demanding to be projected out. The ego, therefore, deals always with the *form*, trying to change things at that level because it does not want to pay attention to the *content*.

Another word *A Course in Miracles* uses to describe the content of Cordelia's response is *defenselessness*; the content of what all our responses should be. We do not have to protect ourselves from attack, since there is no attack, only a *perception* of attack. Please note that I am not talking about *form*, but only *content*. Form (i.e., behavior) will differ from one person or situation to another, but it always follows content, even though the expression of the same content can look very different. *Defenselessness* simply means that you do not have to respond to a perceived attack, because the idea of attack is an interpretation and therefore not what you think it is. Attack, viciousness, dependency, and need for cannibalism start and end with the same thought of specialness: without my special love and hate partners I cannot survive. All forms of attack are born of the same content of fear that made this world and sustains it; the same fear that gave birth to all of us. Jesus explains in the Course that the origin of every dream is fear.

> For every dream is but a dream of fear, no matter what the form it
> seems to take. The fear is seen within, without, or both. Or it can
> be disguised in pleasant form. But never is it absent from the
> dream, for fear is the material of dreams, from which they all are
> made. Their form can change, but they cannot be made of
> something else (T-29.IV.2:2-6).

The forms fear may take within our dreams are often quite horrendous:
vicious, murderous, and totally insane. However, that does not change
the fact of their common origin, nor that defenselessness remains the
only sane response to the world, because it says: "Nothing is happen-
ing to me; nothing has the power to take the peace of God from me.
Whatever the perceived threat might be, it does not affect the reality of
Who I am."

It is that certainty that motivated Cordelia's response. She did not
need her father's special love or wealth, so she could quietly assert the
fact that love is equal: It does not choose *one or the other.* Cordelia's
example is telling us that we can learn how to be silent in the presence
of the ego's raucous screams for specialness, thereby allowing the still,
small voice of the Holy Spirit to speak through us. This does not necessarily mean His speaking through us in words. We simply become
His vehicle for the expression of love in whatever form is appropriate
for the circumstances. His Word is simply love, and our minds give
shape to its expression, which may take the form of words, but the
inner response of the Holy Spirit is always the same: changeless love.
Once again, we are concerned only with *content*, not *form.*

There is no need to change the ego, either our own or the ego we
perceive in others. Once we attempt this, we are making it real and saying the ego is the problem, a perception the ego blesses and fosters.
However, the ego is *not* the problem, and *that* is the ego's problem: it
is nothing without our belief in it. Once we try to change something,
believing that change will bring us what we want, we are falling into
the ego's trap of making the error real, another important principle of
A Course in Miracles. Again, we are not talking about changing what
people do or do not do on the level of behavior. We are talking about
changing the *source* of behavior.

The idea is that before you do anything, you first want to be clear
that you are coming from a place of inner silence, the dwelling of the
still, small voice within. In other words, you want to be sure you are

not acting out of your ego's raucous shrieking or the ego's insistence that there is an external problem that has to be solved; whether the problem is the ego itself or one of its manifestations. The *only* problem that has to be solved is our mistaken choice. Jesus is consistent about that from the beginning of *A Course in Miracles*, and all the way through its three volumes, the two pamphlets, and *The Gifts of God*, the prose poem he had dictated to Helen. The message is always the same: be silent to the ego in order to be present to the soundless melody of the Voice for God within. One of Helen's poems is entitled "The Soundless Song."[2] The idea is to let the Holy Spirit's soundless song express itself through you. It is the song of love, and the fact that it is soundless does not mean that you would not say something verbally. It simply means that what you say from the inner silence has the *content* of love.

The difference between the defensive reaction of the ego and the defenseless response of the Holy Spirit is that the ego always reacts to something perceived as external, while the Holy Spirit knows that there is nothing out there, and therefore nothing to be defended against. This is why, in that original moment, the Holy Spirit did not give a response to the Son, who demanded that the ego and the Holy Spirit respond to the tiny, mad idea. Again, the ego responded gladly and gleefully by telling the Son how wonderful was the idea of separation: "This is what we have always yearned for. Let us rejoice!" On the other hand, the Holy Spirit's reaction was silence, a gentle smile that said: "What tiny, mad idea? What specialness? What individuality? There is nothing there. You but remain at Home, dreaming of exile" (adapted from T-10.I.2:1). The message of *A Course in Miracles* is therefore to help us learn to be silent in the presence of the ego, allowing us to be open to the Holy Spirit and return Home.

---

2. *The Gifts of God,* p. 76.

Chapter 1

HELEN'S POEMS–I

"The Holiness of Christmas"[3]

We will be looking at a number of Helen's poems in our discussion, and we begin with one written on Christmas Day 1973 called "The Holiness of Christmas." It is a nice way of summarizing what we have been discussing up to this point.

> Christmas is holy only if you come
> In silence to the manger, to behold
> Your holiness made visible to you.
> Your gifts are but your open hands, made clean
> Of grasping. Nothing else you lay before
> The newly born except your doubts and fears,
> Your pale illusions and your sickly pride,
> Your hidden venom and your little love,
> Your meager treasures and unfaithfulness
> To all the gifts that God has given you.
> Here at the altar lay all this aside
> To let the door to Heaven open wide
> And hear the angels sing of peace on earth,
> For Christmas is the time of your rebirth

In this and many other of Helen's poems, as well as in places throughout the text, the birth of Jesus becomes a symbol for our own birth. What is meant by *rebirth* or *born again* is the spiritual rebirth that occurs as a result of the miracle when we choose the Holy Spirit rather than the ego. The ego was "born" from the choice for separation, individuality, and specialness, so to be reborn is to choose again. Jesus says to us in "The Holiness of Christmas" what he says throughout *A Course in Miracles*, asking us to bring to him our open hands "made clean of grasping." *Grasping* is symbolic of our special relationships, wherein we are always trying to get something from someone or something outside. To repeat our earlier discussion, specialness results from the thought that there is something wrong within, something missing,

---

3. *The Gifts of God*, p. 97.

something painfully deficient. We seek outside ourselves for a missing treasure—the priceless pearl of our specialness—and seize it when we think we have found it, grasping to replace what we feel is missing inside.

Jesus is telling us the gifts we should offer him, or lay before the Christ child, are the doubts, fears, illusions, and pride that accompany the "meager treasures" of specialness that represent our turning away from the gifts of holiness God has given us. Simply stated, we bring our guilt to Jesus, the guilt that gives rise to the world, which in turn defends against this guilt, as do all strivings for specialness. The source of our guilt is the belief that we have betrayed God by deciding that we do not want His gifts of Love and eternal life. When we choose separation, we throw those gifts away in exchange for the ego's shabby offerings of specialness and individuality. Inevitably what follows is pain and suffering, hatred and death, all of which have their source in thoughts of separation and guilt.

We are thus asked to do what makes Christmas, or any other day holy: bring to the holiness in our minds the unholiness we believe about ourselves. To do this, it is most important to realize that the unholiness is a thought in the mind, not outside in the world. Before we can bring our unholy gifts to the gifts of love Jesus offers us, however, we must first be aware that the unholiness is not in our person, or in anyone else. It is in our minds, which means we must withdraw the projections we placed on others. We must release everyone from the terrible yet illusory burden of responsibility for our unhappiness. In special love, the burden we place on others is that they are responsible for our happiness. That is as hateful a burden as blaming everyone for being the cause of our unhappiness. When we say, "I could *never* be happy in this world if it were not for you," that is just as hateful as saying, "I *would* be happy in this world if it were not for you." Special hate and special love are the same: different forms that express the same content. Either way, we lose.

Forgiveness begins with releasing everyone from the horrible burden we have placed on them of being either a special devil or special savior, realizing that the problem is never outside our own minds. When we become aware that the problem is inside, we can recognize that it is our own guilt for having betrayed God and His Love that results in the different ways we project onto others. It is this guilt we bring to Jesus, but that must begin with honestly looking at what it is we are doing, and how we try to make everyone else responsible for what we secretly believe is our own sin.

"The Ancient Love"[4]

I would like to look at two other poems that make this same point. Both are concerned with forms of silence. The first is not very nice. "The Ancient Love" is basically an indictment of Jesus. Many of you know that some of Helen's poems are concerned with blaming Jesus for her misery, while others acknowledge her love for him; this one clearly is in the category of the former. Here Jesus stands accused by Helen of being silent—not being there for her. This is a clear projection of her having silenced him, and an example of what can be called the ego's silence, which lies buried in all our minds. It involves a deep sense of sin and guilt over what we believe we did to God. We rejected Him, and continue to reject Jesus, but blame *Them* for being absent in our lives. We said to God, in effect: "Your love is not enough. I will find my own, thank you. Your kingdom is not what I need. I will make my own, thank you." The guilt over this perceived betrayal is so horrific that we literally made up a world to hide it, which then becomes a world in which we re-enact the same dynamic of silencing the Love of God. However, now we project our guilt by blaming others, holding them responsible for our being so unhappy and miserable, and atop the list are the two great Abandoners: God and Jesus. Again, in this poem Helen turns her sights to the perceived absent and silent Jesus:

> Love, You are silent. Not one shining word
> Has reached my heart for an eternity
> Of waiting and of tears. I have forgot
> Your face that once was everything to me,
> But now is almost nothing. What You were
> I do but half remember. What You are
> I do not know at all. What You will be
> Is unimagined. Sometimes I believe
> I knew You once. And then again I think
> You were a dream that once I thought was real.

---

4. *The Gifts of God*, p. 44.

25

My eyes are closing, Love. Without Your Word
I will but sleep, and sleeping will forget
Even the dream. Is silence what You gave
In golden promise as the Son of God?
Is this bleak unresponsive shadowland
The overcoming that You offered those
Who understood the Father through the Son?
Is endless distance what must stand between
My Love and me? You promised that You will
Forever answer. Yet, Love, You are still.

I think any one of us could have written that poem. It is a searing indictment of Jesus for not being there for us when we needed him, and for not keeping his promise. However, it is quite obvious, if we were honest with ourselves, that the searing indictment would really be directed within. *We* are the ones who betrayed Jesus, and condemned him to a silent existence in the graveyard of our minds. His love is always present; but we are the ones who silenced it. Our guilt is so horrific and horrendous—there are no words in the English language, or any other language for that matter that can adequately describe such guilt—that we had no choice but to cover it over, project it, and then blame everyone else, including Jesus and God. One could even say that all religions represent an attempt to hide this guilt, either by pretending we believe God is not angry and loves us, or by projecting the guilt, making Him the one responsible for the separation and our misery.

Thus we make God and Jesus into special love or hate partners. In special love They are wonderful. They love us and we love Them—one happy family. But again, this is but a defense against the underlying feeling of guilt that comes from believing we abandoned Them forever. Thus They had no choice but to abandon us. In special hate we say more directly that They do not keep Their promises, loving only certain people or certain groups. Whichever form our projections take, the "God" we end up worshipping is one of specialness.

"Conversion"[5]

This second poem was also written on Christmas Day, the same day
in fact of "The Holiness of Christmas." It is an interesting poem. The
first of its three stanzas refers to the silence of the ego, which we discussed in relation to the first Christmas poem. The next two reflect true
silence: Cordelia's silence, or the silence of the Holy Spirit, which quiets the ego's raucous shrieking. I recall that when Helen had written
down this poem we could not find a suitable title. Helen's original was
"Silences," reflecting the two varieties, but it did not seem to fit. I forget who came up with "Conversion"—Helen or I—but the title fit perfectly once it came to light: the poem's theme of transformation from
the silence of bitterness and death to the silence of peace and eternal
life. That conversion or transformation reflects the shift in our minds
from choosing the ego to choosing the Holy Spirit. Here is the first
stanza:

> There is a silence that betrays the Christ
> Because the Word of God remains unheard
> By those in bitter need. Unspoken still
> The Word salvation holds for them, and kept
> Away their resurrection from a world
> That is but hell and alien to God's Son.
> Homeless they wander, nowhere finding peace,
> Unknown, unknowing, blind in darkness, and
> Unborn within the silence of the tomb.

This is a grim rendering of what our life is really like; a grimness
we avoid facing by saying everything here is really wonderful—happy
things go on in the world, and everywhere are found signs of hope. But
there is no hope in the world because this world is not our home, as we
are told at the beginning of Lesson 182. Each of us wanders in this
world, "unknown, unknowing, blind in darkness." We are homeless
here, but desperately trying to deny what we secretly know to be true.
Even if we do not experience meaning now, we say, I will yet find it.
Or, if I do not have it but others do, it is only because they took it from
me. Therefore my purpose is found in hating them. In one way or
another, we all desperately try to find meaning in a world that is

---

5. *The Gifts of God,* p. 61.

inherently meaningless. In the fourth act, the two friends Gloster and Lear are reunited after enduring great suffering, and they comment on the inane weariness of the world. Gloster says:

> *This great world*
> *Shall so wear outto naught.*

(IV,vi,136)

And Lear a bit later adds his observations on what it means to be born into such a world; our tears are more than appropriate:

> *We came crying hither:*
> *Thou know'st, the first time that we smell the air,*
> *We wawl and cry....*
> *When we are born, we cry that we are come*
> *To this great stage of fools....*

(IV,vi,180,184)

Only one heavy into denial would attempt to dispute this harsh and bitter fact of our earthly existence. After making similar observations in Lesson 182, Jesus states: "No one but knows whereof we speak" (W-pI.182.2:1).

The only meaning this world holds lies in discovering it has no meaning: real meaning is not found in the world, but in the part of our minds we have excluded and betrayed. As the opening lines say: "There is a silence that betrays the Christ / Because the Word of God remains unheard by those in bitter need." In this poem, and many others, as in *A Course in Miracles* itself, the term *Word of God* is a symbol for the Atonement, the principle that states the separation never happened. When we turned away from the Holy Spirit, we buried the Atonement in our minds so that it was silenced. We rejected His silent reminder that there was no tiny, mad idea and therefore there was no separation. The betrayal and guilt we feel are not really about the tiny, mad idea that seemed to arise out of nowhere in our minds. The betrayal was when we chose the ego's interpretation of the tiny, mad idea over the Holy Spirit's; a betrayal we relive over and over when we choose to exclude Jesus from our personal lives, and silence his message of forgiveness and peace.

It is important to underscore this understanding of the nature of our "betrayal," because this will allow us to make the connection in our daily life. Again, it is *not* the tiny, mad idea that is the problem; not the silly, impossible thought of being separate from God. The problem is our having chosen to listen to the ego, which led us to take the idea of separation very seriously and to believe that it was a glorious day when that thought was born—when we received the "gift" of our special-ness. It is that decision for the ego that betrays the Word of God in our minds, and we re-enact its insanity without ceasing. That is the point of Jesus' comment in "The Little Hindrance": "Each day, and every minute in each day, and every instant that each minute holds, you but relive the single instant when the time of terror took the place of love" (T-26.V.13:1).

Any thought of specialness, neediness, criticism, anger, mild annoyance, or any thought that speaks of duality and separation within the Sonship—regardless of the form, large or small—is nothing more than a shadowy fragment of the original ego thought when we betrayed Christ by banishing the Holy Spirit from the kingdom of our minds. That is guilt's source, and everything we have ever done with the ego is nothing more than an attempt to cover the searing pain of that thought of denying Christ.

We undo that thought by not repressing it. Were we to do so and believe that the betrayal is not in us, we would automatically project it and find fault with everyone else. Each time we experience the tri-umph of our specialness, getting what we think we want—we are thumbing our noses at God, saying the love He denied us we can find in this person, substance, activity, work, or whatever. When we have a good feeling from helping humanity and doing such noble work, we are actually telling God that this fulfillment does not come from Him, but from all the wonderful things we are doing. Every time we indulge our specialness, we are likewise telling Jesus to get lost, condemning him to the silent tomb of guilt we made to be his home.

This tomb is the silence of the ego, painful because it means we have thrown away our innocence and will never get it back. Therefore, we have to cover it with the ego's raucous shrieking—the insane sounds of specialness, whether of pain or ecstasy. All this commotion fills our lives—our attempts to find meaning and hope—and is nothing more than our pathetically feeble attempts to cover the emptiness in our minds where love seems absent and the Word of God silent. Only when we become aware that this defense is the problem—forgetting that the world is neither the problem nor the solution—can we go within in search of a better way; another kind of silence.

29

That leads us to the second stanza, wherein we recognize that we need be silent to the ego, not to the Word of God; silent to what we have chosen to silence the Word of God:

> There is a silence into which God's Word
> Has poured an ancient meaning, and is still.
> Nothing remains unsaid nor unreceived.
> Strange dreams are washed in golden water from
> The blazing silence of the peace of God,
> And what was evil suddenly becomes
> The gift of Christ to those who call on Him.
> His final gift is nothing but a dream,
> Yet in that single dream is dreaming done.

The peace of God is a "blazing silence." It says nothing, but simply shines its silent truth.

Most of you will recall the line in the workbook: "We say 'God is,' and then we cease to speak...." (W-pI.169.5:4). Theologians say "God is," and then write volumes! Or a group of people write a book about God called the Bible. We are always writing about God, always talking about Him. It is all unpeaceful noise! Jesus tells us here that we cease to speak when we say "God is" because God is within the silence. It is a state of total silence to the ego and all things of the world. Yet, we fear that silence, and it is that fear that makes it so difficult for us as a society—let alone as individuals—to simply be "still and quietly [do] nothing" (W-pII.1.4:1). The ego tells us that in that stillness God will come, and we will not like what He will say to us: "Think not He has forgotten" (M-17.7:4). The ego has us convinced that we are sinful betrayers, and therefore deserve to be punished for our treachery. The Holy Spirit assures us that when we are inwardly quiet and the sounds of the world are silenced, we will hear the Word of God tell us that nothing has happened: no sin, treachery, or betrayal—"strange dreams," all.

When the poem says "His final gift is nothing but a dream," it refers to forgiveness. "Yet in that single dream is dreaming done" means that the Atonement is the final dream. The Atonement says that what you thought happened never did. Those are not words spoken in Heaven, for there are no words in Heaven. Words are found only within the dream, ended by the words of the Atonement.

In the third stanza, we find a specific reference to Christmas as well as Easter:

What seems to be a birth is but a step
From timelessness to time. The peace of God
Shines down upon a manger and a cross
In equal silence. Neither one will last.
The dream of a beginning and an end
Can never touch God's Son. He seemed to take
A human form and then he seemed to die.
There is no death because there is no birth.
The crucified is risen up to God.

The birth "from timelessness to time" is the ego's "birth," which seemed to involve leaving our true home in eternity to come into a world of separation. When that world was projected in form, it became a world of time and space. But, in truth, nothing happened. There was no birth, no death, no crucifixion—only a dream of birth, death, and crucifixion.

"The crucified is risen up to God" refers to when we awaken from the dream of crucifixion. Here, as we often find in the Course material, *crucifixion* is used to refer to both the crucifixion of Jesus, and the death of God's Son when he betrayed his Identity as Christ, believing He could be separated from His Father.

The great Western myth of the birth, death, and resurrection of Jesus is a re-enactment of the betrayal of Christ, for which we all harbor guilt, along with the hope that somehow, magically, it can be undone. That myth focuses almost exclusively on the body because it represents the realm of magic. In truth, "the crucified is risen up to God" when we awaken from the dream of crucifixion and realize that absolutely nothing happened. We just *thought* we crucified God's Son. We just *thought* we betrayed the Love of God. In truth, it was but a bad dream and that is "the blazing silence of the peace of God." It looks on birth and death—on the manger and the cross—in the same way: "The peace of God / Shines down upon a manger and a cross / In equal silence. Neither one will last."

The Word of God says: "The dream of a beginning and an end / Can never touch God's Son." That dream has nothing to do with Who we are in truth. What do the illusions of birth and death have to do with us? The answer, like Cordelia's, is to love, and be silent. The world answers with a great deal of words: about the meaning of life itself—birth and death, pre-existing life and afterlife, multiple lives, the life of the universe, of galaxies beyond galaxies, a single star, a human being—it is all nothing! The peace of God shines down in blazing silence on all illusions, and nothing need be said, explained, or done. That is the true meaning of *defenselessness*. There is nothing you need do except think differently: to shift from the ego's thought system of betrayal that silences the Atonement, to the thought system of the Holy Spirit's forgiveness that speaks silent volumes of God's peace.

When you strive to do anything in this world in order to make it better, when you strive to make your body or other bodies better, or attempt to heal a relationship, you will fail. The peace of God shines in silence. That does not mean that your body would not do anything in the world. It simply means that whatever your body does—and it may do a lot of things—the *content* behind your doing would be silence. Again, this does not mean you do not speak; it simply means your words would come from silence. All behavior would arise out of the inner silence of the Holy Spirit. Nothing you say or do would be motivated by a desire to say or do. You simply behave in the way love shines through you. You may appear to be quite active in the eyes of the world, but it will no longer be you who are doing anything. That was the meaning of Cordelia's thoughts to herself: "*What shall Cordelia do? Love, and be silent*" (I,i,62). Yet she spoke, and her verbal behavior had profound effects on subsequent events in the play.

In Act Four, Cordelia and Lear are finally reunited, after Lear's horrific humiliation and madness. Finally coming to his senses, he is in prison awaiting execution, as is Cordelia. He comes face to face with the daughter he has so grievously wronged, and says to her:

> *Be your tears wet? yes, faith. I pray, weep not:*
> *If you have poison for me, I will drink it.*
> *I know you do not love me; for your sisters*
> *Have, as I do remember, done me wrong:*
> *You have some cause, they have not.*

Cordelia answers simply:

> *No cause, no cause.*

(IV,vii,71)

In this wonderful scene Lear is telling Cordelia he knows he has sinned against her, has betrayed her love, and therefore she has just cause to hate him. Her response of "*No cause*" tells him he is forgiven, for nothing happened; her love for him has not changed.

You may remember the important theme of cause and effect, which is discussed throughout *A Course in Miracles* (see, for example, T-6.I; T-27.I; T-28.II). Jesus explains that the way you demonstrate there is no sin is to demonstrate that whatever it was, it had no effect on you. That is defenselessness. You demonstrate that someone's seeming sin against you has in fact not affected you in any way. Whatever others have done, or believe they have done, your love for them has not changed one iota; the peace of God in you has not been altered. Thus you demonstrate that their seeming sin against you had no effect, and could not be a cause. That is a simple logical statement. If sin had no effect, it cannot be a cause of anything. Finally, if something is not a cause it cannot exist, because everything must affect something.

That is the basis of the argument Jesus uses to demonstrate that nothing in the world is real. It is not real because it is not a cause of anything. Mind is the only cause within the dream, not the body or anything associated with it. In *A Course in Miracles* "sins" are for-given because they are based on the false idea of separation. If separa-tion is not true, it cannot be a cause and can have no real effect, which means that sin is not real and guilt has no cause. That is the foundation of the Course's unique meaning of *forgiveness*.

In Heaven the principle works the same way. God is First Cause, without a second. His very nature of Love, inherent in His Being, extends. This extension, also termed creation, is His Effect, Christ. Thus is God the Cause, and Christ the Effect, at one with His Creator and Source.

Cordelia, again, provides us with a wonderful example of forgive-ness. She tells her penitent father that his seeming sin against her had no effect. Clearly it had an effect in the world of form. Indeed, it destroyed practically everyone. However, at the end of the play, in which both Lear and Cordelia die, she tells him that because his "sin" had no effect, she has no cause to withhold her love, which never changed, despite his insane rantings and cruel actions. Again, Cordelia shows us what it means to love and be silent. Her other-worldly qualities led her to "allow" such horrific behavioral consequences to unfold, knowing that non-special love alone will remain.

In this world we love to—and not very silently—show others the effect of their sin against us. No head of state has ever waged a war without letting the enemy know the terrible things they have done, echoing the response of the sinned-against God to Adam and Eve:

"Because of what you have done—your sin against me—you will be punished." President George Bush is said to be a religious man, and he echoes the God of his faith as he says to the world: "Because of what you have done, you will be punished." However, he is but the latest in an historically long line of heads of state who have uttered those words. In fact, in one way or another we all say to our special partners: "Your very real sin against me has had very real effects, and so you deserve to be punished." As we read near the end of the text, "'I am the thing you made of me, and as you look on me, you stand condemned because of what I am" (T-31.V.5:3).

Thus when Lear comes before his daughter near the end of the play, he fully expects to be punished by her. He, believing he is undeserving of love, expects to be told of the justified consequences of his sin. He expects Cordelia to say: "How can I possibly love you? Look what you did to me!" We would all be tempted thus, because our lives are based on the principle that sin and guilt are real. When you were an infant, for instance, and your mother did not feed you on time, you let her know in no uncertain terms that her "sin" had an effect. Our lives begin that way, and continue to build on the principle that sin is real and does indeed have real effects on us. We most certainly let others know when they have not met our needs, and make it very clear when we have chosen another to be the object of our guilt, a surrogate we have chosen so that we do not have to be punished for our sins. We are hardly silent in our accusations: my sick body, tortured psyche, and lonely, isolated soul will make sure you know what you have done to me!

In "The Ancient Love," that is what Helen was communicating to Jesus, and that is what we all communicate to God: "If you really loved me, you would not have allowed me to be born into this wretched world. You would have overlooked my sin and not have punished me." We know God punished us, because the holy Bible tells us so. But the Bible tells us that story because *we* wrote it. You must get in touch with the raucous shrieking in your own life that screams out to everyone: "You did this to me!" Above all else you want to demonstrate that another's sin has affected you, and because it affected you it is real: it has caused you to suffer.

Forgiveness-to-destroy is a phrase that Jesus uses in *The Song of Prayer*. It is a subtle example of how we say to others: "Your sin *has* had an effect." It takes the form of expressing to someone: "Yes, you did do a terrible thing, betraying me and destroying my life; but I still forgive you." Jesus goes to great lengths to point out that we cannot forgive something we have made real. When you communicate to others that their "sin" has had an effect on you, you are establishing that "sin" as a *real* cause. It is not possible to erase the cause, after first having made it real. The "sin" can be erased only when you show that it had no effect, and therefore was not a cause of suffering.

Defenselessness is the witness that says: "Your 'sin' against me has had no effect." That means that the seeming sin cannot be a cause. If it is not a cause of anything real, as we have seen, it does not exist. That is how sin and guilt are undone. Real sins are to be punished, but the *belief* in sin is just a belief; a mistaken decision that can be corrected. Thus Cordelia gently corrects her father's mistake by communicating to him that his seeming sin against her is *"No cause."* He was mistaken to believe that Cordelia ceased to love him when he rejected and betrayed her. What he did was simply a silly mistake. Despite what happened in their lives after that mistake, despite the horrendous and painful things that occurred in the world of form, Lear's mind could be at peace, because, in truth, nothing betrayed or destroyed love. Forgiveness such as this is possible only when it comes from a place *outside* the world's dream of pain and suffering, of sin and guilt. That place of course is the right mind, wherein is found the Holy Spirit and His principle of Atonement. Such an understanding is the only thing that makes comprehensible Cordelia's otherwise very strange response to her father at the beginning of the play. As has been said, one should live one's life so that it would make no sense to anyone in the world.

Within that right-minded state of peace, it does not matter what goes on in the world of form; only retaining that peace-filled love is important. You do not worry about fixing the world: saving, healing, punishing, or changing people. All you need do is find peace within your own mind. It is in that peace that the world is healed. It changes when you can look at it through Jesus' eyes, knowing the world is a dream. In order to attain this vision you have honestly to examine your life—day in and day out, moment by moment—so that you can see how it is geared towards *not* silently telling people what they have not done to you. "Love, and be silent" means that you silently identify with the Love of God in your mind. Period. From that silence you speak whatever loving words are appropriate to the situation in which you find yourself. It is not the words—the *form*—that are important, but the quietness of the *content*. If the content of your mind is truly quiet, then it must be that peace is there: "The blazing silence of the peace of God." Sin and guilt are never quiet, although at times the ego can seem to be silent. Yet is it a damning silence. We all know about the "silent treatment," a silence that says: "You have hurt me, and deserve to be punished for it."

Before ending this part of my presentation I want to comment on a concern that is frequently voiced by students of *A Course in Miracles*, and others who read it: If we accept the teaching that our lives are but dreams, does that not foster an apathy that leads to inactivity and uninvolvement in the world? This is a logical and natural concern, and there is indeed a danger of concluding that nothing matters because everything is illusion. But that is most definitely *not* the message of the Course. The danger arises when one slips in the ego under the guise of asking the Holy Spirit what to do. If you practice what *A Course in Miracles* is teaching, it does not mean that you would be apathetic and do nothing. The appropriate emphasis is always on *content*, not *form*. The closing paragraph of the section entitled "I Need Do Nothing" is relevant here:

> Yet there will always be this place of rest to which you can return. And you will be more aware of this quiet center of the storm than all its raging activity. This quiet center, in which you do nothing, will remain with you, giving you rest in the midst of every busy doing on which you are sent. For from this center will you be directed how to use the body sinlessly. It is this center, from which the body is absent, that will keep it so in your awareness of it (T-18.VII.8).

This means that we first go to that "quiet center" in our minds—the place of silence—and from that center we will be guided. Very often this will mean that we return to the world's "raging activity." This quiet center is like the eye of a hurricane, wherein everything is still, despite the fury swirling around us. That "eye" is where the Holy Spirit is to be found, and we can continually return to Him, if we so choose. In fact, we can go there even while occupied in the world of time and space, accessing that silence midst our activity here. It is that quiet center we allow to direct what we do and say.

Very often, the fear of that quietness leads people to distort the message of the Course. People say, for example: "*A Course in Miracles* says this is all illusion and the body is nothing; therefore why should I do anything? If I do anything, I would be reinforcing the illusion." What those people miss is that they are reinforcing the illusion simply by saying: "I don't have to do anything." They would not take this position unless they had first made the error real of believing that *doing* something in the world was somehow wrong or unspiritual. Like many other passages in the Course, the passage we just read is not saying you should not act in the world, but rather that before you act, go first to that quiet center in your mind in which there is no guilt, judgment, or concern.

It is always helpful to keep in mind that *A Course in Miracles* urges us to see the world as a school of learning. The Holy Spirit or Jesus can be our Teacher, but in order to teach, a teacher needs a curriculum and classroom. In learning forgiveness, the classroom is our lives, and the curriculum consists of the relationships and situations in which we find ourselves. If we decide that we do not have to do anything in the world, we are denying our Teacher a curriculum, which is the only means through which we can be taught. A teacher needs a textbook from which to teach and upon which to base assignments. Our lives, again, are the textbook, and so it is important that we do things in the world, because that provides the classroom and curriculum wherein we *un*learn, through forgiveness, the lessons of separation and specialness that we taught ourselves. We can only unlearn those lessons with our Teacher if we first go to the silence in our minds. There alone we find Him, and there alone we allow Him to teach.

Finally, I suggest that you be wary of those who quote *A Course in Miracles* in support of the position that says not to become involved in the world. No one else knows what is the right thing for you to do or not do. But there is a right way of *thinking*: a right way of looking and a right Teacher to consult. When you consult that quiet Teacher, your body will automatically do what is right, unless you are afraid. But when you fear the silence in your right mind and its gentle guidance, there will be a strong tendency to use the metaphysics of the Course as a defense: since the world is an illusion, you do not have to act, or undertake any worldly responsibilities—you simply love, be silent, and do nothing. But to quote another famous statement of Lear's:

O, that way madness lies…

To which we should add his conclusion:

> *let me shun that;*
> *No more of that.*

(III,iv,21)

Chapter 2

"I WILL BE STILL AN INSTANT AND GO HOME"

Let us turn now to the workbook and Lesson 182, "I will be still an instant and go home," to which I alluded earlier. We begin in the middle of paragraph 4. The first part of this lesson discusses how the world is not our home, which I spoke about earlier. The second part starts in the middle of paragraph 4, where Jesus speaks of the Child in us. This theme dovetails with the idea of being silent and defenseless, yet active in the world.

Another important theme of *A Course in Miracles* is introduced here as well: *not making the error real.* Let me say a few words about this before we begin with the lesson. The tiny, mad idea of separation is, of course, an error, for separation from God is not possible. However, when the decision-making Son of God asked for reactions to the tiny, mad idea, the ego responded by taking the idea quite seriously, thereby making it real. The ego told the Son the separation was an actual event, and as it developed its story, separation became a sin and we found ourselves trapped in a multitude of further mistakes. Everything in the ego thought system comes from the original mistake of making the error of separation real and branding it sinful. On the other hand, the Holy Spirit's response to the tiny, mad idea did not make the error real at all. He simply loved and was silent, saying nothing at all because there was nothing to be said about nothing. His defenseless silence spoke volumes, as we have seen, but was not what the Son wanted to hear, anymore than did King Lear.

In this world we make the error real when we are hell-bent—literally—on proving others wrong by having our suffering be a witness to their sin. We make error real by calling mistakes sins, an ego trap Cordelia avoided when she forgivingly said to her father: "*No cause, no cause,*" meaning there is no reason for me not to love you, despite what you think you did to me. She was not making real the error of his vanity and specialness, even though on the level of form these traits certainly brought about disorder, chaos, and pain, especially to people who did not deserve it.

Defenselessness is a response born of the recognition that an error is simply an error; it is not something real because it demonstrates no effect, thereby abrogating the seeming cause. It is obvious from reading *A Course in Miracles* that Jesus does not believe in sin, but if he did he would say that the only sin is making the error real, a mistake which initiated the miserable dream that culminated in the world. Indeed, the physical universe provides seeming witness to the reality of the error that the separation from God actually occurred.

Once again, the Holy Spirit's response to the tiny, mad idea of separation is the exact opposite of the ego's: He gives no response but silence. Any other response would have made the error real. In this connection it is very important to understand that when Jesus speaks in *A Course in Miracles* about God giving an answer to the separation, it is not meant literally. God cannot respond to the separation because it is not real; there is nothing to which He could respond. Listening to the Son's ego, it is the *biblical* God Who responds to the sin of separation—disobedience in the Adam and Eve story—thereby making "sin" real, as the second and third laws of chaos explain:

> The arrogance on which the laws of chaos stand could not be more apparent than emerges here. Here is a principle that would define what the Creator of reality must be; what He must think and what He must believe; and how He must respond, believing it. It is not seen as even necessary that He be asked about the truth of what has been established for His belief. His Son can tell Him this, and He has but the choice whether to take his word for it or be mistaken. This leads directly to the *third* preposterous belief that seems to make chaos eternal. For if God cannot be mistaken, He must accept His Son's belief in what he is [i.e., a sinner], and hate him for it (T-23.II.6).

The attitude of defenselessness, the foundation of forgiveness, lies in not responding to a seeming error or mistake as if it were real. It is important to keep in mind that I am not talking about *behavior*, but an *attitude* or *content*—a thought in the mind. One cannot be truly helpful (T-2.V.18; T-4.VII.8) in this world if one is coming from a content of guilt, or seriousness about a mistake. We can be truly helpful— regardless of the form that help takes—only if we are centered on the content of love, which resides in the silence of our minds. Love is never truly found in behavior, but in the silence of thought that quiets the ego's raucous shrieks: its screaming that something terrible has happened, and we need do something about it. When you believe the ego, you are believing sin is real, with an effect that needs to be undone. However, the only way you can truly be of help is to realize that sin has had *no* effect, which, again, is the message of the silence: the defenselessness of which Jesus speaks in this lesson.

The central figure in Lesson 182 is the Child. The fact that *Child* is capitalized means the word refers to Christ. A passage that we will discuss later says: "Christ is reborn as but a little Child each time a wanderer would leave his home." This does not mean that Christ shrinks to child size. He is spoken of as a Child because in our minds we have chosen the ego, which is to identify with a tiny, individual self. Thus we change our minds in order to grow into our true Identity, our Self. In order to mature spiritually, we need to turn away from the ego and toward another Teacher, another Presence in our minds, to which we listen. It is our spiritual growth that is implied in speaking of Christ as a Child. Again, the Child does not grow: Christ is Christ, spirit is spirit, and They do not age. As we read in the poem "Conversion," there is no birth or death; the peace of God shines equally on the manger and the cross. But we *experience* Christ as a little child that needs care and nourishment, an experience that is reflected here in the world of time and space. Jesus is encouraging us in these passages to nourish this Child in ourselves by nourishing the decision-making part of our minds, reinforcing the choice for the Holy Spirit instead of the ego.

We have been conditioned by our ego identification to be fearful of this Child, and as a result we have built an entire thought system to defend against Him. Nourishing this Child, therefore—choosing the Holy Spirit, Who holds His memory in our minds—requires discipline and practice. We will discuss this further, but let us now begin our discussion of the lesson, starting with the third sentence of the fourth paragraph.

(W-pI.182.4:3-6) Yet there is a Child in you Who seeks His Father's house, and knows that He is alien here. This childhood is eternal, with an innocence that will endure forever. Where this Child shall go is holy ground. It is His Holiness that lights up Heaven, and that brings to earth the pure reflection of the light above, wherein are earth and Heaven joined as one.

The basic premise of this passage, indeed of the entire lesson, is that the world is not our home. We spoke earlier about how our minds are spiritually bankrupt. When we chose the ego over the Holy Spirit, we bankrupted ourselves because we threw away our treasure, just as did Lear when he chose to listen to his two eldest daughters, turning his back on the daughter who truly loved him. To repeat, as the play unfolds Lear becomes literally bankrupt because his two older daughters take everything from him, leaving him with nothing, exactly what has happened to us as a result of choosing the ego. We have become spiritually bankrupt, and so make a world and body in which we seek to regain our innocence by stealing it from everyone else. We recognize this world is not our home when, as *A Course in Miracles* explains, we learn our true home is the abundance of Christ we believe we threw away, leaving ourselves in a state of scarcity and lack. Because we believe this madness, we need to be taught to choose sanity instead. This process of regaining our treasure by learning to choose again is depicted in the Child's growth—from the infancy of living in this world to the maturity of the real world, the reflection of Heaven's love in which "earth and Heaven are joined as one."

(5) It is this Child in you your Father knows as His Own Son. It is this Child Who knows His Father. He desires to go home so deeply, so unceasingly, His voice cries unto you to let Him rest a while. He does not ask for more than just a few instants of respite; just an interval in which He can return to breathe again the holy air that fills His Father's house. You are His home as well. He will return. But give Him just a little time to be Himself, within the peace that is His home, resting in silence and in peace and love.

These are symbolic expressions, the purpose of which is to depict the process of our learning to choose the holy instant, to listen to the Voice in our minds that speaks of Who we are as Christ.

It is because we are still so identified with the ego and do not choose the holy instant often enough, that this experience is so tiny, symbolized by speaking of Christ as a Child. This is Jesus' poetic plea that we spend more time remembering Who we really are, and less time with the ego. On a practical level, this translates into his plea that in each moment of the day we try to be cognizant of how often and intensely we choose the ego, understanding why we do so, and finally to forgive ourselves for having chosen wrongly.

You are terrified of remembering Who you are! You must appreciate how terrifying this is, otherwise you will not be patient and gentle with yourself in this process of learning to choose. Instead, you will demand of yourself that you be perfect and ego free; and then become guiltily upset when you recognize your constant choices for judgment and specialness, all the petty ways you betray Christ and push Jesus out of your heart. You must look at all that, understanding that such insanity comes from desperately trying to protect another child—the child of the ego, the little self you believe you are and have chosen to replace your Self.

Every time we blame someone else for our lack of peace, we are attempting to avoid responsibility for the inner bankruptcy we feel so acutely. We seek to accuse others so that they will be punished for what we secretly believe is our own sin of betrayal. As we saw in our discussion of "The Ancient Love," it is not Jesus who is silent. *We have silenced him*, and behind him is God, Whom we believe we have silenced as well. That is the root of our sin and guilt, which is why their undoing is a process that takes time, and why, again, Jesus speaks of Christ as a little child Who is being reborn in us.

Consequently, we must learn to be kind and understanding with ourselves in this process of rebirth. This will inevitably translate into our being kind and understanding with others, as we realize that the ego things they do represent their fear of knowing Who they are. We all fear that knowledge, so we all do exactly the same thing to everyone else—in *content*, if not always in *form*. Victims and victimizers are equally insane, but behind their insanity is the sanity of the Holy Spirit, which we all share as well. However, we will not get to that sanity until we first see the insanity; we will not get to the true silence of the Holy Spirit's Word of Atonement until we silence the ego's shrieking. It is only when we silence the ego that we can hear that "blazing silence"; and, again, our fear makes this a process that takes time. This theme is continued in paragraph 6:

(6:1) This child needs your protection.

Obviously, Christ does not need our protection; nor does spirit, nor does God. *We do.* This line therefore symbolizes our need to "be vigilant only for God and His Kingdom" (T-6.V-C). We have to be vigilant for all those times we betray the Child's loving presence in our minds and choose against Christ. It is not our true Self that needs protection. Instead, we have to protect ourselves from our mistaken choices, which we do simply by being aware of them.

(6:2-3) He is far from home. He is so little that He seems so easily shut out...

Remember that is what we have done with the Holy Spirit and the memory of our Self. We have so shut Them out that Theirs is barely an audible sound. As we have seen, the raucous shrieks of our specialness have as their only purpose the silencing of that sound:

(6:3) ...His tiny voice so readily obscured, His call for help almost unheard amid the grating sounds and harsh and rasping noises of the world.

Obscuring that "tiny voice" is the *purpose* of the "harsh and rasping noises of the world." As Jesus repeatedly teaches us in *A Course in Miracles*, purpose is everything. There is a reason the world is filled with "grating sounds"—the ego's raucous shrieks of guilt and hate. There is a reason babies cry when they are born (recall Lear's comment to Gloster [IV,vi,184]): they are trying to drown out the pain of the terrible and terrifying memory of feeling expelled from Heaven—the self-expulsion we seek to conceal behind the ego's wall of projection. That is why, as I said earlier, our bodies are always making noises, distracting ourselves through our business of busyness so that the call of the Child remains unheard.

(6:4-6) Yet does He know that in you still abides His sure protection. You will fail Him not. He will go home, and you along with Him.

Here the process of awakening or rebirth is presented in dualistic terms, as though we go home along with the Child. In truth, we *are* the Child, but as long as we are having this nightmare of betrayal—choosing the ego over God—we think dualistically and believe we have a choice. From our decision for the ego arose guilt, and a world of hate and suffering; from our decision for the Holy Spirit arises forgiveness, and a world of peace and healing.

As long as we believe in the ego's world of separation, we believe we can make another choice, which culminates in the ending of the dream. Within the dream it is meaningful to believe we can choose between the ego and Christ. In truth, however, there is no choice, because we never left Heaven or our Self. But as long as we believe we are here, we have to remember to choose this Child. At the very end we realize we are no longer *choosing* the Child; again, we *are* the Child. At that point the Child is no longer an infant; the Child is fully grown, as are we.

(7:1-5) This Child is your defenselessness; your strength. He trusts in you. He came because He knew you would not fail. He whispers of His home unceasingly to you. For He would bring you back with Him, that He Himself might stay, and not return again where He does not belong, and where He lives an outcast in a world of alien thoughts.

This relates to the opening paragraphs of the lesson. It is very important in working with this material that we recognize this world is not our home. This is not the world in which Christ lives, for He is an outcast here. But it is not only Christ Who is an outcast; *we* are as well. One of the painful truths we must look at with open honesty, without judgment, is how comfortable we are in this world, even when we feel so uncomfortable. Strangely, we become comfortable by knowing whom to blame for our discomfort. We may come to recognize, as the lesson says, that this world is not our home, but we do not accept responsibility for being here. We set it up so that we believe that someone or something beyond our control gave us "life." This is perfect from the ego's point of view, for even if we come to see this world for the hell it is, we can still believe it is not our fault.

In order to make any progress with *A Course in Miracles*, we have to realize that not only is the world hell, but that we chose it and continue to choose it. We know we do so because we believe we are here. We still revel in all the hatred we can justify, all the suffering we can inflict on others in self-defense, and all the suffering we inflict on ourselves so that we can point an accusing finger and say: "Behold, me brother, at your hand I die" (T-27.I.4:6). We must honestly look at the vicious part of ourselves that is so self-deceptive it truly believes it can pull off its lie, just as all politicians believe they can pull off the lie that got them elected, and which continues to keep them in office. In addition to realizing this world is not a nice place, we must recognize it is a place we chose, and that we continue to choose, covet, and cherish. Only then will we be able to look at that choice and say: "I do not want to do this anymore." That is what the Child is saying to us by whispering "of His home unceasingly...."

There is a still, small voice that is always, by its very presence, calling to us. It does not literally call to us in words, but its presence as a memory—as a thought in our dreaming minds—is calling to us. That is what the ego is so afraid of. It is brilliant, ingenious, and malevolent in seeing to it that we never return to the point in our minds where we can choose to hear that Voice. That is why there is a world, and why the world is filled with problems we believe are not of our own making. They are always the fault of someone else, beginning with our parents and continuing with figure upon figure upon figure—all of whom take the role of being responsible for our pain and loss of peace. Governments thrive on this dynamic, just as individuals do. We must understand this, otherwise the Child's whispering will go unheard. In order to hear His Voice, we first have to acknowledge to ourselves how much we do *not* want to hear it.

This explains why all students of *A Course in Miracles* have the same experience—if they are honest about it. They study and practice this Course year upon year, and still find themselves falling into the same traps of specialness; still being attracted to the same insane and hostile thoughts that the non-Course world enjoys. We are no different. You must realize that this happens not because you are a bad student, but because you are a terrified one. Again, if you do not recognize how much you do *not* want to hear the silent whispering of the Child, you will never be able to choose to hear it. We must not deceive ourselves, as Helen had sought to do in "The Ancient Love." We must acknowledge that we all experience the same thing: blaming Jesus, God, and everyone else for our misery. It is only, again, when we recognize that we have condemned ourselves to this hell, and understand why we did so, that we can be in position finally to make another choice.

(8:1) When you are still an instant, when the world recedes from you, when valueless ideas cease to have value in your restless mind, then will you hear His Voice.

We could say that the entire Course is geared toward having us choose this holy instant of stillness, which can happen only when we see the ego's ideas of separation, blame, attack, hate, and suffering as valueless. Lesson 133 says: "I will not value what is valueless." This is a significant theme in *A Course in Miracles*. We have placed value on the valueless, just as Lear did when he valued the valueless love of his eldest daughters. Everyone knew that except the old king. He placed value on the special love that his daughters offered him, just as we placed value on the ego's special love that it offered us in the ontological moment. In that unholy instant we chose the love of our individual identity, the separated and autonomous self that believed not only that it could exist apart from God, but that it *must* exist apart from Him in order to have its specialness needs met. There is a poignant scene in *King Lear* that reflects the pain of vanity, when the king recognizes the loss of his specialness. Lear's foolish pride allows him to be humiliated by Goneril and Regan, who are about to strip him of his royal retinue, which began with one hundred, and by the time they are through with him, is reduced to zero. We enter the scene with Regan getting the number down to twenty-five:

> *I entreat you*
> *To bring but five-and-twenty: to no more*
> *Will I give place or notice.*

The proud king responds:

> *Made you my guardians, my depositaries;*
> *But kept a reservation to be follow'd*
> *With such a number. What, must I come to you*
> *With five-and-twenty, Regan? said you so?*

Regan is not persuaded:

> *And speak't again, my lord; no more with me.*

Lear turns to Goneril in hopes of restoring his number to fifty:

> *I'll go with thee:*
> *Thy fifty yet doth double five-and-twenty,*
> *And thou art twice her love.*

But he foolishly put his trust in one even more cruel than the younger sister:

> *Hear me, my lord:*
> *What need you five-and-twenty, ten, or five,*
> *To follow in a house where twice so many*
> *Have a command to tend you?*

And the final ignominy:

What need one?

The failing king makes one final plea:

O, reason not the need: our basest beggars
Are in the poorest thing superfluous:
Allow not nature more than nature needs,
Man's life is cheap as beast's: thou art a lady;
If only to go warm were gorgeous,
Why, nature needs not what thou gorgeous wear'st,
Which scarcely keeps thee warm.–But, for true need,–
You heavens, give me that patience, patience I need!

(II,iv,248)

Shakespeare is making it clear there is no hope for happiness as long as specialness seals our needs. Lear's demands led immediately to his insanity—albeit temporary—and the ensuing tragedy. But only then could he learn that his one and only need was love, represented by the daughter who was always in his heart. Thus his lesson learned, but only after much, much pain.

The lesson can be stated another way: Our true need is getting in touch with how we continue to place value on the valueless. It means nothing to understand this metaphysically. It means nothing if you do not apply the Course's teaching in your personal life, so that you honestly see your valuing the valueless—the idols of specialness you covet and worship—all the ways in which you value the things of the world, and all the ways in which you value hatred and judgment. Even if you hate yourself for having these ego thoughts, you must recognize that you have them because you want them. No one put the valueless thoughts of judgment in your mind but you. And you must see that fact clearly before you can accept the valuable.

We value the valueless on all levels. Only when we realize that the valueless will give us nothing we truly want, will we be motivated to choose what is valuable. Only then will we be able to hear that still, small voice helping us to silence the valueless. Better, we must silence our *wanting* the valuelessness of the world. And this does not refer only to the obvious material things in which "spiritual people" say they are not interested. We must honestly acknowledge the value we place on specialness, both the subtle and the not so subtle. Highest on the list of valueless things we value are our individual selves. Even when we are miserable, how greatly do we cherish this self! We even cherish the misery, because the misery means "I exist." How desperately we cling to that and do not want to let it go!

(8:2-3) So poignantly He calls to you that you will not resist Him longer. In that instant He will take you to His home, and you will stay with Him in perfect stillness, silent and at peace, beyond all words, untouched by fear and doubt, sublimely certain that you are at home.

This is the ego's great fear; the threat that terrifies it. The ego would be finished if we ever allowed ourselves to return to our minds, recognizing the valuelessness of what we chose and the true value of the Voice we rejected, believing we had betrayed It. Once we allow ourselves to hear the lovely melody of the "forgotten song" (T-21.I), to be in the presence of the "Song of Prayer," we will never again choose the harsh sounds of this world, the ego's "thunder of the meaningless" (W-pI.106.2:1). That shift is the ego's fear, and that is why the Love of God so very quickly becomes the *special* love of God: the song of specialness people die to hear. We turn the abstract, non-specific content of the Love of God into something specific, formal, and ritualistic; something we can touch, see, manipulate, predict, and control. Those are all manifestations of the special love with which we are comfortable, because it is the "love" that nourished us, and indeed gave us birth.

Thus it is vitally important to see the subtle ways in which you value the valueless. You must see how this occurs even with *A Course in Miracles*: the insidious ways the god of specialness creeps into your work with the material—making it special by providing it with form and ritual, linking it with this world, making God, the Holy Spirit, and Jesus manageable in forms to which you can relate, control, manipulate, hate, and love as the ego hates and loves. Notice how quickly you move away from what the Course teaches about returning to your mind and changing *it* rather than the world.

A Course in Miracles will become truly valuable to you only when you realize the valuelessness you have placed upon it. The aforementioned lesson "I will not value what is valueless" (W-p.I.133) is most important in this regard, but it must advance from being only a wonderful teaching to one you apply throughout your day. As you honestly apply the Course's teachings without judgment and guilt, you acknowledge what your ego is doing, and why: for the same reason everyone's ego does—*we like being here*. Even when we consciously hate our lives, we still like the hate! If you hate your existence in the world, you are making the error of existence real and will never leave it. If you hate something, you must obviously believe there is something there to hate. Any right-minded person at some point should hate being here, because this world is a sorry substitute for our home. You can truly leave this world only when you look down on it from "above the battleground" (T-23.IV), seeing "its sharp-edged children's toys" of sin (W-pII.4.5:2) and smiling gently at yourself for the insanity of believing you were here, and that you even wanted to be here. The world then will "fade into the nothingness from which it came" (M-13.1:2) as we say this prayer from Lesson 226, "My home awaits me. I will hasten there":

> Father, my home awaits my glad return. Your Arms are open and I hear Your Voice. What need have I to linger in a place of vain desires and of shattered dreams, when Heaven can so easily be mine? (W-pII.226.2; italics omitted)

To reiterate this important point, if you hate the world and are desperate to leave it, you are only making real the error of separation. In Lesson 161 Jesus says: "Hate is specific" (W-pI.161.7:1). There must be something specific as a target for your hatred. Thus if you hate your body you are making the thought of separation specific and real, which is why another line in the text so wisely says: "Who punishes the body is insane" (T-28.VI.1:1). That is because the body is not the problem. Incidentally, we could also say: "Who hates the body is insane." Since there is nothing there to hate, anyone who does so must be insane.

It is not enough simply to say: "I do not hate people anymore, because I realize I hate *me*." If you still hate being here, hate your body and the world, you are expressing your hatred of the separation and yourself for having chosen it. Such hate, once again, makes the separation real. The silence of this hate—buried in our minds—is not the silence of love, but of condemnation. Love does not see error, but looks beyond it to the light of "blazing silence," realizing the error was but a veil that had no power to keep you from the light. Making the error real by seeing sin instead of a mistake, reflects the ego's purpose of turning the flimsy veil into a solid wall that would forever shield you from the light of Heaven's love.

The first step in protecting the Child and allowing Him to grow is the recognition that sin is only a mistake. The ego's solid wall of granite becomes a veil that lacks substance, allowing our vision to see the light beyond it. You must realize that it is as much a mistake to value hating the body and the world as it is to value special love. Both make the error real by having our special love and hate objects become tangible, as the ego silently rejoices. It loves *all* forms of religion, for example, because they make the error real, establishing God as something tangible—or, better, *someone* tangible. Thus is God transformed into a person to whom we can relate, making real the duality of relationship.

Yet because we believe in a dualistic world, we must begin the process of spiritual growth with a dualistic experience of Christ as a little Child. Our purpose thus becomes to let the Child grow up, which means *we* have to grow up, coming increasingly to realize there is no difference between the Child and us. He seems to grow in our awareness; but, of course, this means *we* are growing. We thus begin with duality—where we believe we are—but grow towards the awareness of oneness; a process that seems to take place over time.

(9:1) Rest with Him frequently today.

Remember that this passage comes in the context of the workbook, the purpose of which is to provide a one-year mind-training, or *retraining* program of forgiveness to correct the ego's training of judgment. If you have been through the workbook you know that part of this retraining consists of spending periods of time each day thinking of the lesson and doing what it asks of us. The idea is to train us to spend the rest of our lives with the Holy Spirit as our Teacher, learning there are no distinctions among any of the relationships or circumstances in our day. Each one offers us the opportunity to choose against the ego's conflict, and for the rest that comes through letting go of judgment. Recall these lines from the text: "You have no idea of the tremendous release and deep peace that comes from meeting yourself and your brothers totally without judgment" (T-3.VI.3:1).

Jesus is asking us to spend as much time as we can throughout the day with this Child, and to remember how much we love Him. In the holy instant to which he leads us, we no longer love the things of this world; we no longer love the child of the ego that we thought we were.

In that instant of rest we no longer worship at the shrine of self, trying to make our self better, happier, less sick, or more spiritual. Indeed, the only way we become more spiritual is to realize there is no self that can become more spiritual.

(9:1-2) Rest with Him frequently today. For He was willing to become a little Child that you might learn of Him how strong is he who comes without defenses, offering only love's messages to those who think he is their enemy.

Here again we find the important theme of being in the world without defenses. As long as we believe someone has done something to us and the world is a threat, we make the error real and justify our defenses. It is impossible to exist without defenses in this world, for we need to defend ourselves against disease, starvation, thirst, the elements, and especially against each other. We have to, because that is the nature of the world we made.

However, as we increasingly choose this Child, resting in His Love, we can learn to *be* in the world, yet remembering we are not *of* it. We do everything bodies normally do to sustain themselves, but there remains a part of our minds at rest with this Child. As Jesus describes in Lesson 155: "You do not change appearance, though you smile more frequently. Your forehead is serene; your eyes are quiet" (W-pI.155.1:2-3).

All the while we rest with the Child we are truly defenseless, the condition that comes from recognizing our invulnerability. Cordelia was able to answer as she did—to love, and be silent—because she knew she was invulnerable to anything that might happen as a result of her father's folly and madness. The love she felt for him, and that she knew he felt for her, would be intact regardless of what happened. Therefore at the end of the play she could truly forgive him, saying in effect: "You have done nothing to me." Her love was invulnerable to the silly vanity and specialness in which Lear indulged himself. Only when you genuinely know that you are invulnerable—a knowledge that comes when you rest with the Child within—can you be truly defenseless in the presence of the world's attacks.

Once again, I am not speaking about behavior, but a thought system: *content*, not *form*. Your body might indeed appear to be defending itself, but you remain defenseless in your mind. *A Course in Miracles* is not about behavior, but attitude. You cannot be truly defenseless if you are not coming from a place of strength wherein you rest with the Child. Jesus tells us more than once that we always choose between our own weakness and the strength of Christ in us (e.g., T-31.VIII.2:3). That is always our choice: the weakness of sin and defensiveness, or the strength of innocence and defenselessness.

The strength of Christ lies in His perfect Oneness, Love, and Identity: at One with Himself—undivided, unseparated, unfragmented, unified with His Source. Source and Effect are truly one and the same, and therein lies the Self's strength, which we chose against. We did not want to be part of the One, but separate individuals on our own, wherein lies the ego's weakness.

It is so difficult to choose against our weakness because the ego has taught us our separated self is our strength, a "strength" with which we have totally identified. Yet the defenseless love the ego says is weakness is our true strength. We believe, however, there is strength in individuality, in being autonomous. Indeed, a major value in our society is self-reliance and independence. There is a certain element of truth to that of course; but in back of this value is the original thought of separation when we said to God: "I want to be autonomous and free. I want to be reliant on myself and my strength, not Yours." That "inner strength," however, is actually weakness because it is divorced from the strength of God and Christ.

We all have this pretense of strength. When nations build up armaments, they are flexing their muscles and pounding their chests like Tarzan, saying: "Me Tarzan, me strong!" But underlying this show can only be a thought of weakness; otherwise they would not have to beat their chests and parade their armaments for the trembling world to see. Underneath the chest pounding is the ego's weakness that knows it is nothing without the Son's belief in it. When we choose to separate from God's Love we are nothing, but the ego in its insanity has us believe we are everything.

In order to defend against the weakness and fear that accompany the nothingness of separation, we have devised a thought system—along with a world to support that thought system—that says we are something, and we are something meaningful and significant. Just as the ego has made us "strong" by defeating God and feeding off Him, we make ourselves strong in this world by feeding off others in their defeat and our triumph. Whether we do it as governments or individuals, the theme of all special relationships is triumph. This is inevitable because *ideas leave not their source*, and the source of our individual identity as bodies is the original idea that our individual strength came by triumphing over God. That is why Jesus asks us in the text: "If you perceived the special relationship as a triumph over God, would you want it?" (T-16.V.10:1).

The consequences of this triumph are devastating, if we allowed ourselves to get in touch with them. When we get what we want from someone, there is an initial exhilaration over the victory, but inevitably follows the horrible thought—if only unconsciously: "Oh my God, I did it again!" And then the depression. Similarly, cannibalizing a fifth of scotch and feeling its immediate "wonderful" effects is inevitably followed by a not-so-wonderful hangover.

Jesus is trying to teach us that each and every time we get what we want from someone, or defeat the enemy—whether on an international or personal level—we are re-enacting the ontological moment when we believed we triumphed over God, vowing we would never give back what we took: our individual existence. When we wrote the Bible, we did so that we would have and keep the individuality we stole. Thus our God—not the true God—gives us this individuality. Of course He does! We made Him up, and then told Him what to do. The Bible thus reflects a cult of individuality, which is why it has been such a widely successful book; it justifies individual existence in God's own words and deeds, since He created us. Yet individuality has nothing to do with our true Source, Who knows nothing about it.

The difficulty involved in choosing against our weakness is understandable given our belief that our strength, our very existence as individuals, depends on feeding off other people. That is why the body was made to be in a perpetual state of lack: always needing oxygen, water, food, etc.—its very existence demands it feed off other living things, which reveals its cannibalistic nature. Like the ego itself, the body feeds off other life to maintain its life. That is why governments wage war and economies thrive in times of war; that is why people lust after war and victories. Even when they are defeated, they are victorious because they can use the defeat to justify building up strength for the next war. And on and on and on it goes.

Nations wage war and feed off other nations; businesses exploit and feed off other groups—all because individuals do the same. It is the law of the jungle because the original ego thought has never left its source. In order to live, we must feed off what we call "life." God was the original life and we fed off Him, and it was our devouring that caused His demise. Now He has been introjected and *we* have become God. Devouring to survive is what we continually do, and we must come to recognize that this is weakness, not strength. For that recognition to occur, we first must understand how difficult it is to make the shift from perceiving strength in individuality to resting with Christ. We do not want to lose what we think we have gained through our triumph over others, believing our strength is nourished, sustained, and reinforced by taking from the outside. In our insanity we have chosen this weakness, rather than accepting the strength of Christ within.

Our spiritual growth is a process that takes place over time. Once again, Christ must be reborn as a little Child because we are still so spiritually immature. This is why Jesus continually refers to us as little children. It is only when we know who we are as children of strength, rather than children of weakness, that the Love of God can extend through us to those we think of as enemies, or to those who think of us as enemies. This is difficult because our existence as individuals depends upon, thrives on, and was born from stealing life and feeding off others. That is why we are so resistant to seeing the Sonship as one, and our "enemies" as no different from ourselves, being our mirror images. We feed off them just as they think they feed off us. Even when we lose we believe we gain, for we then become victims. Accusing our victimizers means they will ultimately lose, because blaming them allows us to feed off their innocence, making it our own. It is vital to appreciate the difficulty of this process; otherwise you will not be able to choose the strength of Christ for yourself.

(9:3-4) He holds the might of Heaven in His hand and calls them friend, and gives His strength to them, that they may see He would be Friend to them. He asks that they protect Him, for His home is far away, and He will not return to it alone.

Christ cannot return to Heaven unless we return with Him, because Christ is One. Even though He appears as a little Child, He still "holds the might of Heaven in His hand." Remember, it is only our fear that renders Christ little in our experience and in need of protection.

(10:1) Christ is reborn as but a little Child each time a wanderer would leave his home.

Each time we leave our home in Heaven—each time we reject Christ—we relegate Him to nothingness. It is only when we realize there must be another way and begin our journey back that Christ is reborn in us. He must be reborn as a child because it is a long journey, and our fear ensures our maturation will be slow. In truth the journey is illusory and takes no time at all, yet within the dream it seems almost interminable; our identification with the dream is so intense, and our resistance to growing up unimaginable in its strength.

(10:2) For he must learn that what he would protect is but this Child, Who comes defenseless and Who is protected by defenselessness.

When the decision maker—the "wanderer"—chose the ego, Christ did not fight back or oppose in any way. He did not leap to His feet, raise His hand, and cry out: "What about me?" He just loved and was silent, gently waiting for the insanity to pass, when we would come to our senses and choose Him again, just as in Shakespeare's play Cordelia chose to be silent. Kent, Lear's trusted friend, tried desperately and in vain to stop his master from his folly, knowing the tragedy that would inevitably follow. Cordelia did not even try to dissuade her father, but merely waited patiently—in silence— because she knew the outcome of love would never change.

We all have split minds—the wrong-minded ego and right-minded Holy Spirit—and it is only a matter of time until we make the right choice. Cordelia's spiritual advancement allowed her to wait patiently for the outcome that was as certain as God (T-2.III.3:10). In the play it is clear that Lear had another side to him, by virtue of the love and devotion he received from so many. There is, for example, the interchange between the fallen King and his beloved Kent, now in disguise. Lear inquires:

Dost thou know me, fellow?

The response:

No, sir; but you have that in your countenance which I would fain call master.... Authority.

(I,iv,26)

Yet Lear himself later recognizes how far he has fallen from his erstwhile authoritative wisdom. He says pathetically to Cordelia:

> *Pray, do not mock me:*
> *I am a very foolish fond old man,*
> . . . .
> *You must bear with me:*
> *Pray you now, forget and forgive: I am old and foolish.*
>
> (IV,vii,59,83)

Beyond the foolishness there yet beat the noble heart of one who chose again. Thus Cordelia's forgiveness merely looked beyond her father's foolish detour from the truth, to the shining truth that remained.

One of the characteristics of advanced teachers of God discussed in the early pages of the manual is *patience*: they are patient because they know the outcome. Advanced teachers know their reality is outside time, so they actually wait on nothing. They are patient because they know that eventually the Son of God, like Lear, will come to his senses. Similarly, when we chose in that original instant to betray Christ and reject the Holy Spirit's Word of Atonement, the Holy Spirit and Christ waited patiently for our return. To us it may seem a very long time has elapsed—billions of years in fact. But Jesus tells us in the text: "What is a hundred or a thousand years to Them [Christ and the Holy Spirit], or tens of thousands?" (T-26.IX.4:1). While we wanderers travel the insane journey away from truth, They wait for the time when the pain of our wanderings becomes so great that we finally say: "There must be another way; what I am doing is not working."

Thus Christ waits patiently to be reborn as a little Child, knowing we will change our minds and come home—with Him—to Him. *A Course in Miracles'* purpose is to help us make that change, not because Jesus is impatient, but because he does not want us to suffer any more than we have to. It is a fact that we are all suffering here, yet stubbornly insisting we are right. Yet very often—and this is known by every parent, teacher, and adult who deals with children, including adult children—you have to let people make their mistakes because that will be the only way they can learn. It often is the most loving response to let those in fear devise their own classroom, even ones of hate, failure, pain, and suffering, only because at some point that same classroom will be the vehicle Jesus uses to teach them the other way.

If you deny people the right to change their minds by your attempted intervention, not allowing them to make their mistakes, you deny them the only thing in the world with the power to save them: their mind's power to correct their mistaken choice. The form of their mistake then becomes the form in which they learn the lesson of forgiveness, called by the text our special function (T-25.VI). This is the special relationship through which we learned and taught hate, pain, and guilt, which now becomes the means within which we change our purpose, to undo what we had made. That is why, again, patience is such an important characteristic of the advanced teacher, as is gentleness. Our lesson is to learn that gentle patience with others and with ourselves. Thus does Christ grow from a little Child to adulthood.

(10:3-4) Go home with Him from time to time today. You are as much an alien here as He.

To go home with Christ you must first recognize that you truly are an alien here. Otherwise there will no motivation to set out on the journey.

(11:1) Take time today to lay aside your shield which profits nothing, and lay down the spear and sword you raised against an enemy without existence.

When we look at the situation as described here, we realize the silliness of our lives of defense and attack. We are fighting an enemy that does not exist, yet we remain hell-bent on proving it *does*. We are like Don Quixote tilting at windmills, believing they are the enemy. Cervantes' famous hero is all of us. Whenever we wage war with an external enemy, we are tilting at windmills. We are trying to see the evil enemy outside, instead of recognizing he is within. Until we see the evildoer in our minds, we will not realize there *is* no evildoer. Nothing has happened. We must lay down our shield, spear, and sword because it is our own attacks that keep the ego's thought system strong in our experience.

(11:2-5) Christ has called you friend and brother. He has even come to ask your help in letting Him go home today, completed and completely. He has come as does a little child, who must beseech his father for protection and for love. He rules the universe, and yet He asks unceasingly that you return with Him, and take illusions as your gods no more.

Even though Christ rules the universe—the universe of spirit—in a sense we rule Him because we have the power to choose or reject

Him. This does not have anything to do with Him, but in our minds *we* are the ruler of the universe, as the workbook tells us in Lesson 253. We rule the universe of our minds, our little kingdom, so we can choose Heaven or hell, Christ or the ego, love or hate. *A Course in Miracles* appeals to the power of our minds to choose in which kingdom—the ego's or God's—we will live. It is essential we be aware of what the choice for the ego entails: a kingdom of weakness, pain, hate, guilt, and hopelessness. Until we are so convinced, we will never choose the Kingdom of love.

(12:1-3) You have not lost your innocence. It is for this you yearn. This is your heart's desire.

Many of you know the line in the *Psychotherapy* pamphlet where Jesus says: "And who could weep but for his innocence?" (P-2.IV.1:7). Our tears, pain, and suffering stem from the belief we have thrown away our innocence and will never get it back. They come from our bitter memory of the ontological instant when we bankrupted ourselves. The good news of course is that in truth we are not spiritually bankrupt at all, and have not lost the treasure of our innocence. We simply buried it, and so it is not truly gone but hidden under a massive overlay of guilt and hate, in turn overlaid by a world of specialness and death; we merely closed our eyes to its presence. Still this innocence waits patiently for us to change our minds and hear the Child's call to return home.

(12:4-7) This is the voice you hear, and this the call which cannot be denied. The holy Child remains with you. His home is yours. Today He gives you His defenselessness, and you accept it in exchange for all the toys of battle you have made.

Yet they do not seem like toys to us. We recognize them as such only when we are able to raise ourselves above the battleground, to see with Jesus the insanity of the world. On the battleground, as Jesus tells us at the end of Chapter 27, the world looks serious indeed with heavy consequences (T-27.VIII.8). But when we lift ourselves above it and look down, everything is different. With this little Child beside us—this Child of strength—we see the silliness of all things people do, individually and collectively, throughout history and today. All wars, sufferings, and deaths are but the products of the toys of battle. It does not appear that way from on the battleground, but our perception changes when we rise above it with Jesus by our side.

(12:8-9) And now the way is open and the journey has an end in sight at last. Be still an instant and go home with Him, and be at peace a while.

When Jesus says "be at peace a while," he is acknowledging the fact that this is a *process*, not something we accomplish overnight. You will make a big mistake if you think that you will return home today or tomorrow. In principle of course you can, because this is a journey without distance and without time. But within the illusion of time and space, the world of our resistance to love, time is needed to help us gradually and gently let go of our grip on separation, specialness, and guilt. After all, it took King Lear five acts to come fully to his senses.

Chapter 3

CHRISTMAS PASSAGES

The Holy Instant and Holy Relationships

I would like now to look at a number of passages in the text that deal specifically with the theme of Christmas. These come at the end of Chapter 15, and we begin with "The Time of Rebirth." As one reads through Chapter 15 it is interesting to note how themes related to specialness—especially the idea of sacrifice and its relinquishment—are woven into the discussion of Christmas without breaking stride. We find the same phenomenon near the end of Chapter 19 and the beginning of Chapter 20, taken down at Easter time, where Jesus weaves together Easter themes and his message of forgiveness. Sacrifice is an inherent part of specialness and it is integrally bound up with the principle of *one or the other*: If I am going to get what I want, someone has to be sacrificed. Since I survive by feeding off others, these others become the sacrifice—I win, another loses.

The first passage to be considered is the beginning of Section X in Chapter 15.

(T-15.X.1:1) It is in your power, in time, to delay the perfect union of the Father and the Son.

A major theme of *A Course in Miracles* is that within the dream we have the power to delay the coming of truth. This does not mean, however, that we have the power to affect "the perfect union of Father and Son" in Heaven, reflecting the principle of the Atonement: separation is impossible and never truly happened. Stated another way, within the dream we are free to believe anything we wish, but that freedom does not grant us power to change reality. We merely have the ability—"in time"—to *believe* we could alter reality, establishing our own as substitute for God's. Thus our ability to believe that separation is true does not mean that it is. When we accept the Atonement for ourselves, we will remember the truth of that unbroken union as it dawns on our healed and happy minds.

(1:2) For in this world, the attraction of guilt does stand between them.

It is guilt that says we have separated from God, so obviously it is our being attracted to guilt—wanting it to be real—that keeps us from remembering who we are as God's Son. That phrase, "the attraction of guilt," comes back in spades in Chapter 19 where it is discussed under the first obstacle to peace (T-19.IV-A.i). The attraction can be understood in two ways, both of which are building blocks of the ego's thought system. First, I am attracted to the thought of guilt because it means I am a sinner—betraying God by separating from Him. I have actually done it, so I have made the error real, brought about by guilt. And so I am attracted to anything that will make me feel guilty, reinforcing my self-concept as a miserable sinner, and therefore as a separated one.

Second, I am attracted to guilt in others, thereby protecting myself through projection. This concept is the main burden of "The Attraction of Guilt," the first obstacle to peace. We are attracted to guilt in others, which is why we love to hate. If you are guilty I must be guiltless, following the principle of *one or the other.* You are guilt-full (a word I just made up), establishing me as guilt-less. And so, when God breaks through the massive defense of the world, in hot pursuit of the sinner who betrayed Him, seeking His destruction, He will not punish me because I am guiltless. It is the guilty one— *you*—He shall seek and find. This is the core of our need to project: attempting to get rid of guilt by putting it in others, reflecting the archetypal sacrifice of God so we could live. Now you in turn have to be sacrificed, in order for me to avoid God's wrath—again, *one or the other.*

(1:3) Neither time nor season means anything in eternity.

Jesus is telling us not to put too much credence in Christmas as a *form.* After all, there is no Christmas in Heaven. Moreover, he does not exist in Heaven any more than we do. Christmas is a season in which the *content*—the rebirth of Christ in us—has become lost in the *form* of the myths associated with the holiday. That is why he says:

(1:4) But here it is the Holy Spirit's function to use them both, though not as the ego uses them.

Aside from its commercialization, the Christian world uses Christmas to serve the purpose of commemorating the virgin birth, Jesus' miraculous entry into the world as the Word of God, which obviously makes him very special. Considering Christian theology from the perspective of *A Course in Miracles*, it is clear the Churches got everything wrong at the very beginning, because they made Jesus special, different, and most unique. These words—*special, different, and unique*—are key words in the ego's thought system that tells us that we, the Son of God, are now independent of God and thus are special, different, and unique. We are a miracle in and of ourselves. Just look at what we pulled off. We destroyed God! That is pretty miraculous and impressive!

Christmas has amounted to the worshipping of the idol of specialness. Yet in *A Course in Miracles* Jesus turns it around, so that Christmas now becomes a symbol of *our* birth, which, as we have seen, is really our *re*birth when we choose again. Obviously, this is not something that we do only on Christmas Day, or during the Christmas season. Jesus is simply using the Christmas theme as a symbolic way of reminding us that each and every day our goal should be to choose again. That means being fully in touch with our egos' machinations, no longer trying to justify or rationalize them, but also not feeling guilty about them either. And so, Christmas becomes for us a time not to celebrate Jesus' birth, but rather to commemorate our spiritual rebirth.

(1:5-6) This is the season when you would celebrate my birth into the world. Yet you know not how to do it.

Obviously we do not know how to celebrate Jesus' birth, because right off the bat we make him different and special. And it was not even his birthday! It was all made up. No one knows the actual date of his birth—almost certainly, however, it was *not* December 25th, the feast of the pagan festival of the Saturnalia—if he were born into a body at all. If the core of the Christmas practice is specialness, then clearly we are looking the wrong way for its meaning. "Ask not the sparrow how the eagle soars," Jesus tells us in the text (T-20.IV.4:7), and so we should not ask the "little wings" of specialness to tell us how to fly on the wings of Jesus' eagle of forgiveness.

(1:7) Let the Holy Spirit teach you, and let me celebrate *your* birth through Him.

The Holy Spirit teaches us by doing exactly what Jesus has been teaching so far in these first fourteen and a half chapters of the text: helping us understand the ego thought system—its foundation and purpose, and how it fulfils that purpose throughout our lives. In this part of the text *sacrifice* is one of the key themes of Jesus' teaching, and he wants us to understand its meaning of *one or the other.*

(1:8-9) The only gift I can accept of you is the gift I gave to you. Release me as I choose your own release.

Jesus is certainly not the only one who has given this gift of forgiveness to the Sonship, but we will remain with him since he is the focus of our curriculum. His gift demonstrated there is but one Son, and the separation never happened. He is witness to the fact that there is a reality outside our dream, the core of which is the truth of the Atonement principle: the separation from God's Love never occurred. There can be no true Love in the dream, but Jesus is, for us in the Western world, its symbol or reflection. Such reflection is the call to join with Jesus in our minds and leave the dream.

When we make Jesus special, we make him an intrinsic part of our dream of specialness. Understandably—given the purpose of the world—the world has brought Jesus into the dream and worshipped him there. We all, as a collective ego, participated in this because *we* wanted to remain within the dream. His "real" presence within the dream ensures that we do so.

To recap: The dream began with the idea we were separate individuals. That thought of individuality encased itself in a body, and so Jesus must be an individual body as well. Since our egos need Jesus as an idol of specialness, he must be made into a very special individual, which means he has something we do not have. Following the laws of the ego's thought system, if Jesus has something we lack, the question arises: "Where did he get it?" Not surprisingly, the ego has an answer: "If I am without the Love of God, which Jesus has, he must have deprived me of it." The ego's law of scarcity operates on the principle of lack, which through the dynamic of projection becomes the law of deprivation. Scarcity comes from the sense there is something lacking in me, and deprivation tells me it is not my fault: someone or something else deprived me of what is missing.

In the Western world we do not have to look very far to find out who deprived us of the Love of God. It was obviously Jesus! That is why he says we do not know how to celebrate his birth: we do not know what it really means. For us it means that specialness reigns supreme. In truth, however, Jesus releases us from our dream of specialness, but he cannot do so until we release *him*. It goes without saying that he is not imprisoned by our dreams of specialness, but he cannot help us as long as we deny his help by dragging him into the dream. His help can only be from *outside* the dream, for the ego cannot be undone from within its thought system, but only from a thought system outside itself. Since we do not want to abandon the ego, we drag Jesus into its thought system, making him an integral part of it.

The biblical Jesus is the one who has been brought into the ego's dream of separation and specialness. That is why he is such a popular figure. The traditional image of Jesus represents everything we think we are. As long as we see him within the dream, he cannot be of help to us because we are asking help of the sparrow instead of the eagle, an idol instead of the true symbol of love. Remember, an idol is a substitute. We have substituted the world for Heaven, the ego for God, and the dream figure of Jesus for love's symbol in our minds. By making an idol of this dream figure, we have ensured that Jesus cannot help us in any way. That is why he says to us in the text: "Forgive me your illusions, and release me from punishment for what I have not done" (T-19.IV-B.8:1) Earlier he says: "I am made welcome in the state of grace, which means you have at last forgiven me. For I became the symbol of your sin, and so I had to die instead of you" (T-19.IV-A.17:1-2).

Thus it is important that Christmas be a time that represents *your* rebirth, which means you ask Jesus to help you be born again: *to choose differently.* We bring to him our grasping hands; those pitiful images of ourselves—our "secret sins and hidden hates" (T-31.VIII.9:2). We bring these to him so he can exchange our "gifts" for his gift of love and oneness: the true gift of Christmas.

(1:10) The time of Christ we celebrate together, for it has no meaning if we are apart.

There are two levels of understanding this statement, both of which are very important. The first is that we not be apart from

Jesus, in the sense that we exclude him from our lives. He asks us to bring our problems to him—*in our minds*. If you ask Jesus to help you in this world, you will never know his true help. You may have the illusion of help, but how can he, who is outside the dream, help you within the dream? Jesus' purpose is to help you *awaken from the dream*. As he told Helen, ask him instead to help you remove the conditions that led to your fear, conditions that always entail a willingness to be separate and, specifically in that example, to be separate from him (T-2.VI.4:3). Jesus was always asking Helen to let him help her; and he makes the same plea to us.

On the one hand, therefore, we have to work with Jesus to let go of our ego, but as we grow in this process and become increasingly silent to the harsh dictates of the ego, we begin to experience his love and hear the silent sound of his voice. At that point we realize, at the second level of understanding, that we are not separate from him at all. At the very end of the journey we realize that we and Jesus are one. Neither of us retains the name we had before. We are one because God has only one Son. However, before we realize we are one with Jesus, we first have to accept that we are separate from him in time, but that he can yet help us learn and grow, beginning as a child and maturing until we become like him. At that point we *know* we are one.

Thus, the idea of not seeing Jesus apart from us can be understood, first, in terms of the early stages of the journey, where he asks us to bring our problems to him to allow their darkness to disappear in his light, and second, in terms of the later stages where the goal is to mature to the point that we know we are not apart from him because we are one.

(2:1) The holy instant is truly the time of Christ.

The holy instant is that instant outside time, in which the decision-making part of our minds chooses Jesus as our teacher instead of the ego. We choose our identity as Christ in the time of Christ, rather than as the ego self in the time of specialness.

(2:2-3) For in this liberating instant no guilt is laid upon the Son of God, and his unlimited power is thus restored to him. What other gift can you offer me, when only this I choose to offer you?

If there is no guilt laid upon anyone, including ourselves, all that remains is the Atonement principle. This must be so because guilt was made to shield us from the Atonement, which says the separation never happened. Remember, guilt is a statement that says the opposite: "I am guilty because I am a sinner, and I am a sinner because I have separated."

In truth, there is no guilt, sin, or separation. In the holy instant there is only the remembrance that we never left home. In the holy instant, which is the "time" we choose Atonement over separation, there can be no guilt. We are told later in the text that in the holy instant there is no body, literally no body: "At no single instant does the body exist at all" (T-18.VII.3:1). In the holy instant there is no experience of the body because the body is the embodiment of separation, a symbolic form of the separation thought. Our minds are healed, at least in that instant. However, this does not necessarily mean the body disappears physically, but only that it disappears in our awareness. That is why we are so afraid. We think: "If I am not my body, who am I?"

Turn now to Chapter 15, Section XI, "Christmas as the End of Sacrifice." This is a continuation of the Christmas theme, and here again we see how Jesus weaves the Christmas theme into what he has been teaching us about sacrifice and special relationships.

(T-15.XI.1:1) Fear not to recognize the whole idea of sacrifice as solely of your making.

This is extremely important. Recall that the idea of sacrifice *is* the principle of *one or the other*, which gave rise to me as an ego, to this existence that I call my self. Moreover, I came into existence at God's expense; and now I continue to exist at your expense. This is why we secretly love to hate, criticize, make judgments, and find fault with others; why we love to be the innocent victims of other people's cruelty, insensitivity, lovelessness, and uncaringness. To protect our selves, we have to prove that someone else is to blame for our misery.

The ideas of *one or the other* and *sacrifice* reflect the children's game of seesaw: someone is up, the other is down. If I am to rise, you must fall; if I am to be sinless and innocent, you must be sinful and guilty. That is the ego's game, and it tells us that God plays that game better than anyone else: He will always win, and we but His sacrificial victims. The notion that God demands sacrifice is found throughout the Bible. Someone must pay the price—sometimes he is evil, sometimes he is good; it makes no difference. God's bloodthirsty need for vengeance is insatiable, and must be fulfilled. Clearly, this has nothing to do with the true God; we speak only of the ego's mocking caricature. The belief that God demands sacrifice because of what we believe we did to Him has literally driven us from our minds in terror.

Thus Jesus says to us here in the text: "This idea of sacrifice has nothing to do with God, Who knows nothing about it or the ego. You are the one who made all this up. It was you who ordained that sacrifice be true, and then called it sacred. This has nothing to do with your Creator, for it is of your own making. Since you are the one who made sacrifice, you have the power to change it; since you are the one who chose wrongly and listened to the teacher of *one or the other*, you can just as easily make the correction and choose the Teacher of Atonement."

(1:2) And seek not safety by attempting to protect yourself from where it is not.

We think safety is in the world and the body. The ego wants to keep itself safe, and it is protected by our remaining mindless. If we do not know we have a mind, there is no way we can ever change it about the ego. That is why the ego believes it can be kept safe by our remaining focused on the body: keeping it safe, secure, healthy, protected, nourished, happy, and free from pain. If these efforts do not work, we can still believe we suffer because someone else did it to us, and that works, too. That is why Jesus advises us not to seek safety where it is not, but only where it can be found: the part of our minds wherein he dwells.

(1:3-4) Your brothers and your Father have become very fearful to you. And you would bargain with them for a few special relationships, in which you think you see some scraps of safety.

Here we see that the safety of the body is always sought through some special relationship, which seems to protect us physically and/ or psychologically. I fear you because I hate you; and I hate you because I think you have what I lack. I have no choice then but to kill in order to get it. My murderous thoughts engender so much guilt that I project them out, forgetting that I have done so. I thus think you are out to kill me:

> ...those who project are vigilant for their own safety. They are afraid that their projections will return and hurt them. Believing they have blotted their projections from their own minds, they also believe their projections are trying to creep back in. Since the projections have not left their minds, they are forced to engage in constant activity in order not to recognize this (T-7.VIII.3:9-12).

If this sounds familiar, it is because it is a classic description of paranoia, from which, I am sorry to say, we all suffer. The ego thought system, as it is set out in *A Course in Miracles*, is that of a *paranoid schizophrenic*, though Jesus does not use those terms. So if someone asks what the Course has taught you, you can reply: "I am a paranoid schizophrenic."

Yet there is hope. But before I can change my mind—the source of all hope—I first must admit to what it is I believe: everyone is out to get me. Why? Because I am out to get everyone else. Since everyone is a split-off part of myself, I must see in you exactly what I see in me, but wish to repress. I deny the murderousness within my mind, project it out, and then believe the sin resides in you. Once I perceive you as the murderer, I am understandably afraid, necessitating a defense against you.

We are all murderers. We believe this to be a fact because that is how we got here: destroying God in order to become who we think we are—at least that is what the ego tells us. It does not reveal, however, that this tale of murder is made up. Our bodies testify that our experiences here are real. As long as we so believe, the only way we could have gotten here was to kill off God. That is the thought of our betrayal through attack and murder; the thought of sacrifice, which remains deeply buried in our minds. Thus the ego tells us the only way we can survive is first to project that thought and make a cosmos, and then fragment the thought into an almost infinite number of pieces, each of which becomes a suitable object for potential projection. Thus we wind up walking this earth in terror that the world outside is going to do to us what we secretly believe we did to God. Recall this important passage from the text:

> The world you see depicts exactly what you thought you did. Except that now you think that what you did is being done to you.

The guilt for what you thought is being placed outside yourself, and on a guilty world that dreams your dreams and thinks your thoughts instead of you. It brings its vengeance, not your own.... The world but demonstrates an ancient truth; you will believe that others do to you exactly what you think you did to them (T-27.VIII.7:2-5; 8:1).

Since most of us act in relatively civilized ways most of the time, our desire to kill others before they kill us needs to be sublimated into more subtle psychological ways. The interested reader can consult the sections of the text on special relationships, particularly in Chapter 16. In the special love relationship we try to steal from the other what we want. Since I usually cannot steal what I want without killing you, I resort to more covert means of getting my needs met: cajoling, seducing, manipulating, and deceiving you into satisfying my needs, all of which is necessary because I am convinced you will not give me what I require for survival unless I give you something in return. This is the special relationship bargain, but we need not delve any further into it now. It is enough to recognize that that is where we all end up: bargaining for the little scraps of what we think offers the comfort of protecting us from our guilt. Thus we settle for scraps instead of the full banquet. At the heart of the ego's machinations is the secret thought we have betrayed God and, more specifically, Jesus, our teacher and friend.

(1:5) Do not try longer to keep apart your thoughts and the Thought that has been given you.

In Chapter 4 of the text Jesus talks about dissociation (T-4.VI.4). We split off the right mind—the Holy Spirit's Thought of Atonement—from the wrong mind, choosing to be aware only of the ego's thought of separation. The purpose of *A Course in Miracles*—to state it in still another way—is to bring the darkness to the light, the ego's illusions of specialness to the truth of the Holy Spirit's forgiveness, the little thought of the ego to the Thought of the Atonement. That is the referent of this sentence. In other words, we do not change the ego thought system, but simply look at it by bringing it to the Holy Spirit.

(1:6) When they are brought together and perceived where they are, the choice between them is nothing more than a gentle awakening, and as simple as opening your eyes to daylight when you have no more need of sleep.

Jesus can make this statement only because he is outside the dream. Within it, however, this choice is not so easy, as we all know. Above the world's battleground, to which he continually invites us, the choice between the Holy Spirit and the ego is not difficult: "Who with the Love of God upholding him could find the choice of miracles or murder hard to make?" (T-23.IV.9:8).

A choice between thoughts of specialness and the thought of real love is simple when they are seen clearly for what they are. When we recognize the painful consequences of being an individual and juxtapose the thought of individuality with that of perfect oneness, the choice is hardly difficult. However, we have *genuinely* to recognize that individuality is painful and distressing, knowing it is no longer what we want. That is what is so difficult, and why it is so hard to look at the ego without judgment: we know if we do, therefore not taking it seriously, it will disappear, and ultimately our self along with it.

When one looks at the consequences of that original choice for the ego instead of the Holy Spirit and sees where it has led, when one can make the causal connection between suffering and the decision for separation, choosing against the ego is very easy. When one clearly sees that the decision to choose separation and join with the ego is the cause of all the pain and suffering in the world, as well as in our personal worlds, choosing again is as easy as a "gentle awakening." People will not continue to bang their heads against a wall when they make the causal connection between the head-banging with blood dripping down their faces, and the tremendous pain they feel. Our problem in making the cause-effect connection is that the ego, in its clever ingenuity, has placed a gap between banging our heads against the wall and our experiences of pain. And so we do not really know why we have such pain, and why the blood is streaming down our faces. A huge gap has been introduced—the world of time and space—between the *effect*, our suffering and pain, and the *cause,* the decision to make the ego our teacher instead of the Holy Spirit.

As our teacher, Jesus wants to help us shrink the gap so we can see the direct causal connection between our decision to be separate and the pain and misery we feel. However, the ego's strategy has been carried out so brilliantly that practically no one has made this connection, which explains why the world has continued on without any real change. Alcoholics need to learn that if they take a drink there are going to be serious consequences. Likewise, if I am a diabetic I need to learn that if I eat a piece of cake there are going to be consequences as well, and I will not have to wait long to experience them. Thus we need to learn that if we manipulate another person into giving us what we want, there are going to be consequences we do not like. That is why choosing Jesus as our teacher would be most helpful. His purpose, again, is to have us see the connection between our decision-making minds and suffering bodies. It is not to treat the symptom and make us feel better. All that he and the miracle do is help us see the connection between our pain and its cause. Only then will we be motivated to stop the masochistic behavior that leads to such incredible pain and suffering.

Sometimes we repeat behavior that led to pain in the past because of the payoff in doing so. Strangely and perversely, the payoff is the misery, actively supported by the ego in hopes that we will turn to it for help. Our sagging feelings are bolstered by the ego's words: "Let us find another relationship. This time it will be different. I promise you!"

More often than not, when we experience the head pain, with blood streaming down our faces, we conclude that someone else did it. The ego tells us who, and instructs us to find and punish the person. But the pain does not stop. For a brief moment it feels good to blame someone else and have them suffer as much as we. Yet the throbbing continues, as does the flowing blood, and we do not know their true source. We still think someone else has done it to us.

The way we are reborn is to see clearly that our pain is caused by our own decision. The decision to change now becomes inevitable. No one, aware of the consequences, willingly chooses to bang his or her head against a wall. We persist in such self-destructive behavior only because we do not know *we* are the ones doing it. That is why, at the beginning of this section, Jesus tells us that we made up sacrifice. That is also behind his words to Helen and all of us in Chapter 2:

> If I intervened between your thoughts and their results, I would be tampering with a basic law of cause and effect; the most fundamental law there is. I would hardly help you if I depreciated the power of your own thinking. This would be in direct opposition to the purpose of this course (T-2.VII.1:4-6).

Jesus is telling us not to ask him to fix the *effect* of a problem in the world. If he did, we would never recognize that *we*—our decision-making minds—are the *cause* of our problems. If we do not recognize that *we* are the cause, we will never change our minds. Jesus cannot help us as we wish him to, for the symptoms are but illusory projections of the problem. Living better in the dream will not help us to awaken, and the miracle's purpose is to lead us gently to the mind (*cause*) where the dream (*effect*) began, so we can make another choice. *A Course in Miracles* is about nothing else.

(2:1-2) The sign of Christmas is a star, a light in darkness. See it not outside yourself, but shining in the Heaven within, and accept it as the sign the time of Christ has come.

These are wonderful lines, the meaning of forgiveness! Do not see the light outside your mind; do not see the solution to your problems where it is not, but see them "shining in the Heaven within, and accept it as a sign the time of Christ has come," signifying the advent of your rebirth. You have accepted Christ and finally acknowledged the little Child we read about in Lesson 182. You have decided to bring this Child home with you, which, as we have seen, means bringing yourself home.

As long as you believe salvation is external—somewhere in the dream—you will never realize the star of Atonement shines within your mind. It cannot be found in the body—in sacrifice, as both the Christian Churches and Judaism have taught; nor can it be found in another person or in ritual. Only by going within will it be yours, and it is accomplished when you look within your mind to see the ego in action, perceiving the direct connection between the cause and its painful effects. Choosing the Christmas star is then easy, as easy as "opening your eyes to daylight."

However, as we all know, there are times when we do not open our eyes and awaken. Unfortunately, that is the spiritual condition we find ourselves in almost all the time. Rather than awaken from the dream and greet the light, we strive to bring the light into the dream, thereby remaining in the darkness of illusion. We thus bring the star of forgiveness into the world, rather than opening our eyes to discover happily that the star has always been within us.

(2:3) He comes demanding nothing.

"He" is Christ. Think of this as a direct parallel to what we just read in Lesson 182: "This Child comes demanding nothing."

(2:4-5) No sacrifice of any kind, of anyone, is asked by Him. In His Presence the whole idea of sacrifice loses all meaning.

What it means to be reborn, for Christ to come, is that we choose Him, meaning we choose against the ego thought system and the raucous shrieking of the special relationship that demands and demands and demands. Ultimately, it demands someone's death. In "The Christ in You" Jesus describes how, following the guidance of specialness, we want to take our brother and hurl him over a precipice (T-24.V.4). In terms of *content,* Jesus means that literally. Most people are too heavy to lift up physically and hurl to their demise, but in thought it is quite easy. We want to kill everyone before they kill us: *ideas leave not their source,* and the ego was born through sacrifice and murder.

One of the ways we sometimes attempt to prove our "love" for others is that we sacrifice for them. Parents love to sacrifice for their children, and then throw it up in their faces. Lovers do that as well: "I love you—look what I have given up for you." When you read the horrific biblical stories about sacrifice, realize that you are reading *our* story. We actually believe that God wants us to prove our love for Him by sacrificing what we hold most dear, as in the story of Abraham and Isaac. Not to be outdone, the biblical God sacrifices what He holds most dear in order to prove His love for us; seen in the Suffering Servant songs of Isaiah, and Jesus, His beloved Son. What insanity! If love is to be truly itself, it must be total: all-inclusive without sacrifice of any kind. The rock on which salvation rests, as we learn in Chapter 25, is that no one loses for anyone to gain:

> The Holy Spirit has the power to change the whole foundation of the world you see to something else; a basis not insane, on which a sane perception can be based, another world perceived. And one in which nothing is contradicted that would lead the Son of God to sanity and joy. Nothing attests to death and cruelty; to separation and to differences. For here is everything perceived as one, and no one loses that each one may gain (T-25.VII.5).

That is how Jesus interprets the meaning of Christmas. If Christ is to be reborn—if we are to choose the little Child—it can only be by choosing against the ego thought system of *one or the other*: "kill or be killed" (M-17.7:11).

(2:6-7) For He is Host to God. And you need but invite Him in Who is there already, by recognizing that His Host is One, and no thought alien to His Oneness can abide with Him there.

We all have thoughts that are alien to the Oneness of God and Christ. Whenever we exclude anyone from our love, whenever we make judgments about anyone, we are excluding not only that person but ourselves. In a sense we are crucifying Christ all over again, because Christ is the one Son of God, Whose Oneness is perfect and therefore must include all its seeming fragments. The ego would have us break this Oneness into billions of pieces. We then pick and choose which ones we like and which we do not. The ones we like, we cherish; the ones we do not like, we kill.

When you read the various stories of God in the Bible, keep in mind that this is the God of the ego. He saves the ones He loves; punishes those He does not. Sometimes He even kills the objects of His displeasure. All this demonstrates the insanity of this God of sacrifice and specialness; hardly the loving Creator Jesus presents to us in *A Course in Miracles*. Again, the point—central to the Course—is that we cannot be reborn in Christ, as Christ, if we violate the Oneness of God's creation.

(2:8-9) Love must be total to give Him welcome, for the Presence of Holiness creates the holiness that surrounds it. No fear can touch the Host Who cradles God in the time of Christ, for the Host is as holy as the perfect Innocence which He protects, and Whose power protects Him.

Love is total, and *that* is our protection. Holiness is the presence of total love, who we are in truth. There is no separation, exclusion, or judgment. As you practice forgiveness day in and day out, observe how often you exclude someone. We are not talking about form, because on the behavioral level you cannot include everyone. However, watch how often you exclude on the level of thought or content. Do not crucify yourself for this, but do not ignore it either. Simply acknowledge to yourself that this is what you do, because you are replaying the original betrayal of God's Oneness. Observe yourself without judgment, and everyone else as well.

As I have said many times, we cannot know we are part of the Oneness of Christ until we first know that we are part of the oneness of the ego. It is essential to realize how we all share the same insanity before we can move beyond it to understand, accept, and truly know we share the same holiness. We are not different—in Heaven or on earth. We are all alike, and that is very important to understand. There is only one evildoer in the universe, and that is us. There is only one holy person in the universe, and that is us, too. There *is* no one else. Within our split minds each of us has a Hitler and a Jesus: We are both the epitome of the wrong-minded thought system of hate and murder, and the right-minded thought system of the Atonement. Both are in our minds, awaiting our choice.

(3:1-2) This Christmas give the Holy Spirit everything that would hurt you. Let yourself be healed completely that you may join with Him in healing, and let us celebrate our release together by releasing everyone with us.

The message of Christmas—"love, and be silent"—is that before we can hear the Holy Spirit's silent Voice, we must first be silent to the ego's shrieking voice of specialness. That is the meaning of "give the Holy Spirit everything that would hurt you." By giving it to the Holy Spirit Jesus does not mean blindly giving it to Him, saying: "Please take it because I do not want it." He wants us to *look* at it. Truly giving it to the Holy Spirit means honestly looking at the ugliness, murderousness, and destructiveness in ourselves, taking responsibility for our choice, recognizing as well the cost to us of such a wrong-minded decision. The meaning of Christmas is our rebirth, the answer to the birth of the ego. We make the transition from the ego to the Holy Spirit by looking, again, with open eyes at what it is we have chosen, and why. We look without guilt, judgment, and the need to protect our decision through projection. We look honestly and say: "I do not want to do this anymore."

We must therefore look at our specialness and be silent to it; no indulging or cherishing it, no seeking to change or deny it. We simply look and recognize our mistake. And that is all. Seeing clearly the choice before us, we correct our mistake, healing our individual minds. This means we are no longer individual minds, as is reflected in the workbook lesson: "When I am healed I am not healed alone" (W-pI.137). This is Jesus' point here, too. We celebrate our release and oneness with Jesus by releasing everyone. This clearly implies that we cannot be with him *unless* we bring everyone with us, without exception.

The process of forgiveness requires that you go through the roster of people in your life that you want to exclude. Usually it is not very hard to do that, but remember not to come down hard on yourself because you still want to exclude certain people from love. At the same time, do not attempt to justify, rationalize, or spiritualize your ego's decision. Simply acknowledge that has been your wish. This should come as no surprise because it is as natural for you to hate as it is to eat and sleep. It is as natural for you to hate as it is to breathe, because the oxygen that keeps the body going is simply a form of the ego's oxygen of hate that keeps it going. Remember that projection protects guilt, and that is the ego's bread and butter. It is the ego's safety because it means you no longer see the guilt in yourself, but in others. When you see it there, you are not aware of it in yourself and so you can do nothing about it.

It is no surprise, therefore, that you project guilt all over the place—hating, criticizing, and taking sides. Of course you still believe there are winners and losers in life, and are happy when your side wins and upset when your side loses—just as you are at a football game. War is no different than a sports event. Observe how quickly you take sides in a situation, and do not indulge your guilt by feeling bad about it. But at the same do not pretend that you do not do it. Of course you do! We all do. Reflecting our first decision for the ego, we continue to project guilt over and over and over again. We take sides in life because we did at the very beginning. The idea is to see that this is what we do, and to see the painful effects of our decision.

It is very important to bring the effect to the cause, so they are no longer split off from each other. As painful as it might be, it would be a wonderful thing for you to have an angry thought and immediately get sick—just like that! If that happened with regularity (which it does, except we do not see it), then you would let go immediately of your specialness thoughts, seeing their painful consequences. If you really could experience the consequences of your hate, judgment, specialness, and exclusion—directly feeling a pain in your stomach, head, spleen, or appendix, or feeling anxious and depressed—you would know and understand the connection between cause and effect. You would then say, and mean: "I do not want to do this anymore—it hurts *me*." Our problem is that we are so good at putting distance between the effect of our pain and its cause—the decision to separate and hate—that we do not know where the pain is coming from, and therefore cannot meaningfully act to undo it.

Again, this is not a course in helping you avoid looking at the ego, or covering it over. Rather, its purpose is to expose the ego, seeing its viciousness and hatred. Only in this way can you learn to see the immediate effects of your decision, the prerequisite for letting them go.

(3:3) Leave nothing behind, for release is total, and when you have accepted it with me you will give it with me.

This is similar to what Jesus means in "The Final Vision" at the end of the text when he says this lovely line: "Not one illusion is accorded faith, and not one spot of darkness still remains to hide the face of Christ from anyone" (T-31.VIII.12:5). At that point we would have forgiven everyone, perceiving not one spot of darkness in another because there would no longer be a spot of guilt's darkness in us. That is what Jesus is telling us here, not to mention throughout *A Course in Miracles*.

"Leave nothing behind, for release is total" means that if you are going to be truly free from the pain of your existence here, from the pain of your wrong decisions, you must let go of your mind's guilt. You learn to do this by looking at your projections, thereby bringing them back within. That is why it is so important to monitor the content of your mind and be vigilant for your hostile thoughts—whether about the day's news or a person with whom you work or live. Watch all specialness thoughts, which would keep you separate and different, but without feeling guilt about them. In fact, you should feel gratitude for being able to observe those thoughts, because that is the only way you can be healed.

(3:4) All pain and sacrifice and littleness will disappear in our relationship, which is as innocent as our relationship with our Father, and as powerful.

Jesus is asking us to look clearly at our relationship with him. If we believe he sacrificed himself for us, and thus believe he is asking us to sacrifice ourselves for him—which naturally entails pain—there is something very wrong; if we see ourselves as little in relationship to his greatness, there is something very wrong. We cannot be healed as long as we perceive Jesus as different. Clearly he is different *in time*, but the purpose of accepting that difference is to have the willingness that would allow him to teach us to become like him. Differences in time are superficial and temporary by definition. Their only useful purpose is allowing Jesus to bring us to where he is: in our minds, the locus of his help. You may recall this passage at the beginning of the text, where Jesus emphatically makes this point:

> Equals should not be in awe of one another because awe implies inequality. It is therefore an inappropriate reaction to me. An elder brother is entitled to respect for his greater experience, and obedience for his greater wisdom. He is also entitled to love because he is a brother, and to devotion if he is devoted. It is only my devotion that entitles me to yours. There is nothing about me that you cannot attain. I have nothing that does not come from God. The difference between us now is that I have nothing else. This leaves me in a state which is only potential in you.
>
> "No man cometh unto the Father but by me" does not mean that I am in any way separate or different from you except in time, and time does not really exist (T-1.II.3:5-4:1).

We can grow to become like him only if we bring all thoughts of victimization, pain, sacrifice, and littleness to his healing love. This is such an important topic, and one so frequently asked about that I want to spend a little more time on it before continuing with my commentary.

Let me say first that it is not necessary for a student of *A Course in Miracles* to have a personal relationship with Jesus. It can be very helpful, to be sure, but what alone is important is to experience a relationship with some symbol—Jesus or any other—that reflects the loving *source* behind the *symbol* of Jesus: "The name of Jesus Christ as such is but a symbol. But it stands for love that is not of this world" (M-23.4:1-2). It is especially important that this relationship not be a *special* one, as the Churches have done for two thousand years, one example being their insistence that unless we confess Jesus Christ as our Lord and Savior we will not be saved. How antithetical it would be to everything Jesus teaches us in the Course if a relationship with him were the only way we could find God!

That being said, it is almost impossible for someone growing up in the Western world not to have some kind of relationship with Jesus. It does not matter whether you were born a Jew, Christian, or atheist. Jesus is such a prominent symbol in the West that he is a presence in all of our minds, whether we believe in him or not; a symbol that in some way or another has to be dealt with. And since his presence in *A Course in Miracles* is so apparent, I think someone would have to do vigorous mental gymnastics to blot him out entirely. After all, much of the Course is written in the first person—Jesus being the source of the material—and there are several references to the biblical crucifixion and resurrection.

Developing a relationship with Jesus is accomplished the same way we practice any aspect of *A Course in Miracles*: we reach the positive by undoing the negative. Forgiveness—the Holy Spirit's answer to the ego's dream of sin, attack, and guilt—is nothing positive in and of itself. It is an *un*doing, as are the miracle and salvation. Developing a relationship with Jesus thus *un*does the relationship with the ego. At some point in one's work with the material it would be helpful to look at how one thinks and feels about Jesus. Chances are there will be many negative associations—special hate or special love: the "bitter idols" described in the clarification of terms (C-5.5:7). Therefore, one develops a relationship with Jesus by working at it indirectly, through letting go of specialness. Forcing a relationship with him will not work, but letting the thoughts and feelings about him surface—without interference—will. The true relationship with him, most likely already there, will simply be itself.

One of the reasons *A Course in Miracles* gives us a choice between teachers—the Holy Spirit or Jesus—is that the former is relatively abstract, whereas the latter is specific. To practice the Course it does not matter whether you choose the Holy Spirit or Jesus, as long as you go within and ask for help from the non-ego presence in your mind. However, once again, the prominence of Jesus in the material behooves students of *A Course in Miracles* to include him as part of their forgiveness lessons. He represents the special relationship, just as one's parents, siblings, lovers, spouses, children, and friends do. Therefore, it becomes almost silly to exclude Jesus in one's practice of the Course; he is part and parcel of the material. I suggest you approach your relationship with Jesus in the same way you would approach any relationship: bringing to the surface all the negatives of specialness, regardless of their form.

Therefore, when I say it is important to develop a personal relationship with Jesus, I am speaking generically, meaning that it is important to develop a relationship with your Inner Teacher. The name you give It is irrelevant as long as it is the One Who represents your right-minded self. But do try to include Jesus as part of the process of looking at your thoughts and feelings about the Inner Teacher.

Now we can return to "Christmas as the End of Sacrifice":

(3:5-6) Pain will be brought to us and disappear in our presence, and without pain there can be no sacrifice. And without sacrifice there love *must* be.

Love came first, then our sacrifice of love, synonymous with the belief in *one or the other*. This belief is our ego's defense against love, the breeding ground for pain. The one who is sacrificed feels pain, and we who sacrifice the other must feel the pain of guilt for having done so. As we have already discussed, we inevitably fear that the other person will do to us what we did to them. And so there is pain and suffering all around, "enjoyed" by everyone. When Jesus says that "pain will be brought to us and disappear in our presence," he means that we will join with him and become like him. As he tells us in the clarification of terms, we then become his manifestation in the world (C-6.5:1). When we join with Jesus, our darkness, fear, and specialness are brought to love and then disappear, exactly as happened with King Lear and his daughter. It just took a while, and great deal of pain, before Lear could accept it.

Love, therefore, is silent and defenseless. It does not do anything, and if we try to make it do something it merely becomes part of the darkness for us. When the darkness is brought to the light of love, the light does nothing. It simply loves, because that is light's nature; love simply loves, because that is its nature. And so when the ego's darkness is brought to the light of love, it must disappear. When we are defenseless, allowing ourselves to love and be silent, we demonstrate that the seeming sin of another has had no effect. That is how we learn this Course; and that is how we learn that our sins are forgiven. When we demonstrate that a seeming sin has had no effect, we are demonstrating it is not real because it is not a cause of anything; therefore the "sin" does not exist—i.e., it is forgiven. To become like Jesus means that when pain is brought to us it disappears in our presence, because in joining with him we represent the non-ego thought system, which simply shines the ego away. Love does nothing else; it does not heal symptoms, or effect physical change. It is simply present. Our function is to join with Jesus, and as we teach his defenselessness, we learn it.

A Course in Miracles explains that to teach is to demonstrate (M-in.2:1). It is not one special person imparting knowledge to another. The interaction takes the form of two separate people, but it is really about demonstrating and learning oneness, wherein teacher and pupil join in sharing the goal of transcending the form that would keep them separate, learning that worldly differences are superficial. The text explains this common goal of teaching and learning our inherent sameness:

> A good teacher clarifies his own ideas and strengthens them by teaching them. Teacher and pupil are alike in the learning process. They are in the same order of learning.... Every good teacher hopes to give his students so much of his own learning that they will one day no longer need him. This is the one true goal of the teacher (T-4.I.1:1-3; 5:1-2).

When we represent the non-ego thought system that says nothing happened, we simply love and are silent. Our defenselessness says nothing happened: there is nothing to be forgiven because there was no sin. This is the meaning of true forgiveness: *there is nothing to forgive.* Recall that *A Course in Miracles*' definition of forgiveness is that you forgive your brother for what he has *not* done (W-pII.1). Whatever he has done on the level of form has not taken away your peace. He has not shattered the Atonement; he has not crucified God's Son. In his insane dream he might have done a great deal, but what does that have to do with you? Your peace is thoroughly protected by what it is, and is invulnerable to what is not itself. In other words, you are not part of the dream of attack. That is why Jesus asks us not to share our brother's dream of sickness (T-28.IV). This does not mean not responding in an appropriate, loving, and helpful way on the level of form, but it does mean that on the level of content—the mind—you are not pulled into the dream. Whenever you get angry, depressed, or exhilarated, you have already allowed yourself to become part of an alien dream.

This, then, was Cordelia's message to her father at the beginning of the play: Love does not get pulled into the dream. Gently and defenselessly it remains silent. Cordelia stood outside her father's dream of specialness; and out of love—clearly an other-worldly love—she allowed him to run the full range of his insanity and folly. In the end Lear learned through that classroom what it means to have sins forgiven, while Cordelia did absolutely nothing but love him. To repeat—the act of loving in the presence of attack says: "There is no cause; nothing happened. Your sin had no effect." That is the true message of Christmas, and that is how we are reborn as Christ. By reflecting the love that is outside the dream of time and space, separation and attack, we demonstrate its reality midst the world of illusion.

Interestingly, near the end of the play Lear reverses the teaching/ student role by saying these wise words to his daughter:

> When thou dost ask me blessing, I'll kneel down,
> And ask of thee forgiveness... (V,iii,10)

This is reminiscent of Hamlet's words to his mother in the dramatic scene when he confronts her with the fact of his father's murder:

> And when you are desirous to be blest,
> I'll blessing beg of you. (III,iv,172)

Shakespeare's point is that the way one is forgiven is to forgive. The healed mind of God's one Son heals all: by withdrawing one's projections onto another, one can then let go of the guilt within that is the source of all unforgiveness. The close of the *Psychotherapy* pamphlet makes the same point about "God's simple ways":

> You were lost in the darkness of the world until you asked for light.
> And then God sent His Son to give it to you (P-3.III.8:12-13).

Turn now to paragraph 8.

(8:1) Let no despair darken the joy of Christmas, for the time of Christ is meaningless apart from joy.

Obviously, this is a world of despair. It is important to look at the despair so you do not deny its presence in your mind. Before you can truly experience the joy that is within you, you must remove what blocks it. If you do not think this world is a despairing place, you are simply not paying attention. The world of bodies *is* a world of suffering, pain, and death. It has nothing going for it, and it must be that way because *ideas leave not their source.* That is what is meant by the passage in the workbook that states: "The world was made as an attack on God" (W-pII.3.2:1). It was made as a defense to protect the guilt that protects the sin that represents an attack on God. The world is simply the final step in the ego's strategy to protect us from the God whose loving Oneness the ego has taught us we have destroyed, and would destroy us in return.

The source of the world is the thought of separation from God, which leaves us in a state of bankruptcy and despair. Remember: "...who could weep but for his innocence?" (P-2.IV.1:7). We are in despair because we believe we will never retrieve our innocence. We made the wrong choice and now the door is closed, and that is that!

To restate this: The world is a place of despair because it comes from the despairing thought "I destroyed Heaven and I can never return." I am thus left with a bankrupted self, and all I can do is steal from everyone else's bank, which of course is as bankrupt as my own. That is true despair, true hopelessness. This is our world: a place of darkness because it comes from a thought of darkness—the thought of being absent from the light of Heaven. Despite the artificial light of electricity, not to mention the sun, the world is *not* a place of illumination.

But hope lies in the very fact that the world is not what we think it is—neither solid nor real. Substanceless, it cannot have been created by God. It is but a projection of a tiny, mad idea about something that never happened. *Ideas leave not their source*: that is the good news. One is reborn as Christ when one looks at the ego thought system at its source—not at the world, but at the *source* of the world. Then one can say and mean: "This is the silliest thing I have ever heard! Who in his right mind would ever have chosen this?" All of a sudden a light goes on and the recognition dawns: "Obviously I was *not* in my right mind! And that's all."

This is the meaning of "Let no despair darken the joy of Christmas, for the time of Christ is meaningless apart from joy." In this illusory world, joy is discovering truth, which means learning that there is no meaning here. The real meaningfulness of the world lies in learning the lesson that the world is totally meaningless. Being totally unreal, it has no power to conceal true reality from us, the only place where true Meaning can be found.

In other words, real joy—the only joy in this world—is learning you are forgiven. That is joy, because your existence has been based on the thought you are beyond forgiveness; the enormity of your sin and horrific nature of your guilt ensure they could never be undone. Even if God wanted to forgive you, He could not because your sin is beyond the power even of Heaven to forgive. The world was made to keep that terrifying thought hidden and to protect us from our guilt. Our joy, then, is in learning that sin, guilt, and fear are made up. There is nothing to forgive because nothing ever happened.

(8:2) Let us join in celebrating peace by demanding no sacrifice of anyone, for so you offer me the love I offer you.

Telling Jesus that you love him is an absolute lie if you do not at the same time bring to him all the people you hate, excluding no one. "Let us join in celebrating peace by demanding no sacrifice of anyone" means that any time we have a critical or judgmental thought—let alone a hateful one—we are demanding sacrifice of someone. We are thinking that because of someone else we are not peaceful; and underneath is the thought that this other should be killed because of what he or she did to us. This thought sometimes breaks through, although most of the time we do not let ourselves experience it directly. The way we offer and receive Jesus' gift of love is to let go of all barriers to that love. Remember his words in the Introduction to the text:

> *The course does not aim at teaching the meaning of love, for that is beyond what can be taught. It does aim, however, at removing the blocks to the awareness of love's presence….* (T-in.1:6-7).

The blocks referred to are the grievances we harbor towards others; the projections of the unforgiving thought that we are the guilty sinners who betrayed God. We demonstrate our love for Jesus not by doing the workbook perfectly; not by studying the text—reading it over and over, memorizing its metaphysics and quoting chapter and verse. Rather, we demonstrate our love by bringing him all our forms of unforgiveness towards others and ourselves. We do this while at the same time realizing there is a part of us that is still grasping our ego. We give with one hand, and take back with the other. Bring that to him, too. Do not try to change anything. Do not try to be holy. Do not try to be spiritual. Simply look at your ego and let Jesus help you do so without judgment. Thus you offer him the love he has offered you.

(8:3) What can be more joyous than to perceive we are deprived of nothing?

If I am deprived of nothing, then I have everything. In other words, to accept that I am deprived of nothing is to undo the belief that someone has deprived me of my innocence. Our real joy—true hope and salvation—comes in realizing I did this to myself, for now I can do something about my despair. There is that line from the text, well-known to almost all students of *A Course in Miracles*, that expresses this thought: "The secret of salvation is but this: that you are doing this unto yourself" (T-27.VIII.10:1).

That is the Holy Spirit's "secret" and our joy, because now at last there is real hope. If someone else did it to me then I have to change that person; I have to find and destroy him, so that he never does it again, as well as seeing to it that his son and grandson never do it, either. I need always be on my guard that someone does not do me— a thankless, unrewarding, and unforgiving task if there ever were one. Someone should tell our government officials that they will never find every terrorist. Why? Because *everyone* is a terrorist. Terrorists are not just hiding in the caves of Afghanistan, the deserts of the Middle East, or the hills of South America. How naïve! Everyone is a hate-filled terrorist. Everyone is a murderer. Only when you realize that *you* are the murderer can there be hope, because *that* you can do something about. You cannot do something about the multitudinous universe, but you can do something about your mind. The joy of salvation is that "you are doing this unto yourself." Therein lies our hope.

A Course in Miracles is filled with hope because it is absolutely hopeless about the world. It cannot be said often enough that real hope comes only when you "seek not outside yourself" (T-29.VII), but see it in the only place where it can be found: your mind. That is the *true* good news—the most hopeful words that have ever been written. This gospel message makes no empty promises that there is something hopeful in the world or body. What could be more joyous than to know you are deprived of nothing, and that no one has truly done anything to you?

(8:4) Such is the message of the time of Christ, which I give you that you may give it and return it to the Father, Who gave it to me.

We return that message to the Father by sharing it with the Sonship, since God has only one Son. There are many places throughout *A Course in Miracles* that speak of God's Oneness, which embraces His one Son. Thus, for example:

> If God has but one Son, there is but one God. You share reality with Him, because reality is not divided (T-10.III.10:1-2).

> …here, before the altar to one God, one Father, one Creator and one Thought, we stand together as one Son of God. Not separate from Him Who is our Source; not distant from one brother who is part of our one Self Whose innocence has joined us all as one, we stand in blessedness, and give as we receive (W-pI.187.10:2-3).

As there is only one Son, the message of non-deprivation—the opposite of *one or the other*—has to be given to all. This occurs at the level of the mind, where I exclude no one, knowing there *is* only one. When my mind is healed, therefore, the Sonship is healed. Jesus is not waiting for everyone to accept the Atonement. We have *already* accepted it. Our problem is that we do not know that yet. Thus when our minds are healed, we realize the Sonship is one and no one is outside that oneness:

> Heaven is not a place nor a condition. It is merely an awareness of perfect Oneness, and the knowledge that there is nothing else; nothing outside this Oneness, and nothing else within (T-18.VI.1:5-6).

(8:5) For in the time of Christ communication is restored, and He joins us in the celebration of His Son's creation.

Jesus explains early in the text that "creation and communication are synonymous" (T-4.VII.3:6). In Heaven there are no separate persons to communicate with one another. The communication

Jesus speaks about is the song he describes at the beginning of *The Song of Prayer*:

> ...the single voice Creator and creation share; the song the Son sings to the Father, Who returns the thanks it offers Him unto the Son. Endless the harmony, and endless, too, the joyous concord of the love they give forever to each other. And in this, creation is extended (S-1.in.1:2-4).

That is creation: Love being Itself. Unfortunately we must use words that are dualistic—"symbols of symbols....thus twice removed from reality" (M-21.1:9-10)—because we are communicating at the level of duality. But we should not be taken in by symbols, which point to a reality that is beyond them, the theme of "Beyond All Symbols" in Chapter 27. When our minds are healed and we are reborn as our Self, all that remains is the Oneness of Christ, and His Oneness with God.

(9:1) God offers thanks to the holy host who would receive Him, and lets Him enter and abide where He would be.

In this part of the text there is a play on the words *host* and *hostage*. We are asked whether we would rather be *host* to God or *hostage* to the ego. Of course it is the mind's decision maker that is being addressed: "Would you be host to God by choosing the Holy Spirit, or will you be held hostage by choosing the ego?" Jesus teaches us that when we choose the Holy Spirit we are choosing to become a host to God. In truth, of course, God does not thank us; this is but a lovely and symbolic way of expressing an idea for which *we* will be grateful when we finally choose a different Teacher.

(9:2-3) And by your welcome does He welcome you into Himself, for what is contained in you who welcome Him is returned to Him. And we but celebrate His Wholeness as we welcome Him into ourselves.

The Wholeness of God is the Wholeness of His Son, which means that we must exempt no one from that Wholeness. That is the key idea in all of this, and that is how we end the thought system of sacrifice.

(9:4-5) Those who receive the Father are one with Him, being host to Him Who created them. And by allowing Him to enter, the remembrance of the Father enters with Him, and with Him they remember the only relationship they ever had, and ever want to have.

Earlier in this chapter Jesus talks about the only real relationship we have, and that is with God (T-15.VIII): the relationship we believe we severed forever. We deal with our sense of lack by seeking to get back what we threw away in attempts to join with special partners, but never finding the unity and love we so desperately want. We do not know where to look, because by identifying with the ego we have closed off our minds, and only there can love be found.

This next paragraph was written after Christmas, just before New Year's Day. It is *A Course in Miracles* version of a New Year's resolution:

(10:1) This is the time in which a new year will soon be born from the time of Christ.

Jesus is using the specific images of New Year and Christmas, but he is really talking about our choosing the holy instant: the time of Christ when we reject the ego's child of hate, choosing instead to be reborn as a little Child, the Christ. Jesus is asking us now to take that holy instant and extend it so that it becomes constant in our lives, not just a single point in a day, week, month, or year. He uses the symbol of the new year to invite us to enter into the holy instant of rebirth by choosing him as our teacher instead of the ego, and then to have the forgiveness born in that instant extend through us by embracing the entire Sonship, as often as we can, day in and day out.

(10:2-3) I have perfect faith in you to do all that you would accomplish. Nothing will be lacking, and you will make complete and not destroy.

This is a reference to what the ego thinks and does, where everything is lacking so that I have to sacrifice someone else in order to fill what is missing in me. Of course, when I succeed, I have in effect destroyed what I now possess, reminiscent of how the ego began: destroying God to fill our lack. We wanted our independence, autonomy, and freedom, and since God would not meet our special need, He had to be sacrificed. We are speaking here on the collective ontological level. On the individual level of our personal experience we seek to end our scarcity by undergoing a long, laborious, and unending search for completion— seeking to be made whole by joining with others, substances, or anything outside ourselves that would satisfy our need. That is why the special relationship never, ever works. It cannot work because it cannot complete us. Only the remembrance of God can do that.

The preceding lines introduce an idea that will be developed much more fully in the next chapter in the text. For instance, in "The Choice for Completion" (T-16.V) Jesus explains how by choosing forgiveness we undo all thoughts that interfere with awareness of our inherent completion as God's Son.

(10:4-7) Say, then, to your brother:

> *I give you to the Holy Spirit as part of myself.*
> *I know that you will be released, unless I want to use you to*
>   *imprison myself.*
> *In the name of my freedom I choose your release, because I*
>   *recognize that we will be released together.*

You have to say this to *every* brother, not just certain special ones. You must release *every* brother, especially those whom you are tempted to exclude. Since special love and special hate are the same, your forgiveness must embrace both those you believe you hate, *and* those you believe you love and therefore seek to cannibalize.

Each and every time you are tempted to accuse someone, you should say this prayer, though not necessarily literally. If you are serious about loving Jesus, really serious about taking his hand and awakening from this nightmare, the only way you can do so is to take everyone with you—not in form, but in your thoughts. If you exclude anyone, you are saying you do *not* want to return home; your love for Jesus is so fearful, his hand the last one you wish to hold. You should look at that dynamic within yourself with honesty and without guilt, judgment, or rationalization. Simply admit: "Yes, this is where I am; I am still too afraid." Such a realization is very useful information to have. The problem is not out there, but in you. It is not a sin, but simply the fear of losing your self, and that mistake calls for correction, not punishment. At this point you are being honest, and that is what Jesus is talking about earlier in the text when he says, "Be very honest with yourself in this, for we must hide nothing from each other" (T-4.III.8:2).

Gratefully, you do not have to pretend you are holy. Earlier in this chapter Jesus says: "The necessary condition for the holy instant does not require that you have no thoughts that are not pure. But it does require that you have none that you would keep" (T-15.IV.9:1-2). There is a huge distinction being made here. Jesus is saying you do not have to have totally pure thoughts. That would be an impossible demand to make of us; no one here has totally pure thoughts. But when your thoughts are impure—thoughts of hate, separation, and specialness—Jesus is asking you not to hold on to them, but to bring them to him. This is all he asks: to be aware of the necessity to preserve your own existence by excluding certain people. And, once again, do not judge yourself for doing so.

(10:8-10) So will the year begin in joy and freedom. There is much to do, and we have been long delayed. Accept the holy instant as this year is born, and take your place, so long left unfulfilled, in the Great Awakening.

This refers to the plan of the Atonement, which, as we have learned, is not a specific plan that assigns us special people, as well as very specific, very important, and very holy work to do. The plan of the Atonement is: *Forgive*. And that is all—dull, boring, same-old-same-old forgiveness. That is the "Great Awakening." That is the great plan. That is how God's one Son awakens from his dream of separation and fragmentation.

(10:11) Make this year different by making it all the same.

That is a lovely line. We "make this year different" from all the others by seeing every situation, relationship, and circumstance as the same, because they *are* all the same. Everything is an opportunity for us first to project our unconscious guilt onto other people or situations. We then ask for help to withdraw our projections, recognizing that what we saw outside is a mirror of something we first saw inside. The darkness of sin I perceived in you is simply a projection of the darkness of sin I made real in myself. And now that I know what I did, I can change my mind. Very simple!

Seeing every day and every circumstance as a learning opportunity makes your life much, much easier. It also provides your life with the only meaning it has: returning to the decision-making part of your mind to release yourself from guilt by asking Jesus to help you look at its source, as well as how you sought to escape its pain by projecting it onto someone or something else. By returning the guilt to where it truly is, you recognize that you no longer have to hold on to it.

(10:12-14) And let all your relationships be made holy for you. This is our will. Amen.

Our relationships are made holy by the removal of all unholy thoughts of specialness and guilt. Again, we remove them simply by looking at them with Jesus. We need do nothing else.

Students sometimes wonder whether there can actually be a relationship between two people in the absence of the specialness that is the basis of most intimate and romantic relationships. In other words, it seems as if without guilt, deprivation, and sacrifice—the core of specialness—relationships here would be impossible. In one sense that is true. But first remember that a holy relationship is a state of *mind*, and has nothing to do with the body. Also keep in mind that "this is a course in cause and not effect" (T-21.VII.7:8), mind and not behavior. This understanding opens the door for *all* forms of relationship: parent-child, spouses, lovers, friends, etc. People can remain in physical relationships that are holy, because there is the commitment, in at least one of the two people, to letting go of the special relationship bargain of trading with each other to meet personal needs. In this world it is unlikely that that would be the case all the time, although the ideal is that it would be.

Thus, when speaking about relationships one must emphasize that the holy relationship is a *process*, not an entity in and of itself; a process of shifting the *purpose* of the relationship from the ego's goal of guilt and separation, to the Holy Spirit's goal of forgiveness and joining.

As we have discussed, relationships are not between two persons, but exist only in the mind. As one learns to let go of sacrifice and the need for specialness, one can only be with another person in the peace in which there is no friction. Egos would claim this is boring, but how can peace be boring? Holiness, therefore, does not mean the end of relationships in this world. Rather, it means the end of the ego's purpose for a relationship. In this shift it is not a question of *one or the other*; the process of forgiveness is experienced as a gradation. In reality a relationship *is* always either holy or unholy. But in our worldly experience, again, the shift from special to holy relationships is a process of moving from the ego to the Holy Spirit. Indeed, that process itself *is* the holy relationship.

Relationships do not just disappear when this shift occurs. It is possible that the two people would remain together in form, but relatively free from the tension and friction that usually characterizes relationships—the highs and the lows. The relationship would be more even, and the focus less on the external and more on the internal; more awareness of the unity of purpose that is present—not in form but in the mind. It is that awareness that keeps the relationship calm and peaceful.

Needless to say, a holy relationship takes hard work, and it succeeds only to the extent that one is intent on shifting one's focus from the other person to oneself. When difficult moments arise, one sees the relationship as an opportunity to get in touch with some darkness in oneself. That does not mean you must bodily stay in a relationship for such opportunities, but you would understand that the ultimate purpose of everything—including the current difficulty—is to help heal yourself. The relationship is not about how the other person is bad or good, mean or wonderful. Its meaning is to help you shift your focus from outside in, from the body's needs to the mind's forgiveness. This shift in focus allows you to see the relationship as the means of healing, or correcting your faulty decision for the ego.

Chapter 4

HELEN'S POEMS–II

"The Resurrection and the Life"[6]

I want to turn back to Helen's poetry in *The Gifts of God*. As many of you know, these were poems that Helen started writing down during her scribing of *A Course in Miracles*. The first half of them, with one exception, were written during the period between her taking down the workbook and manual for teachers, and the last half came after the Course's completion. In different ways, they all share thoughts and themes from *A Course in Miracles*. Helen felt, however, that writing these poems was different from taking down the Course. In the poems she felt that she had a more conscious say, her voice speaking with Jesus, "a collaborative venture" (T-4.VI.8:2), if you will. In fact, in some of the poems the "I" is Helen, while other times it is Jesus. Because of the nature of the "scribing," Helen felt more of a freedom to change the poems than she ever did with the Course, but she did not really do so, other than some very minor editing if she felt that the meter were not quite right, or she did not like a phrase or word. Essentially, though, the poems came through her the same as did *A Course in Miracles*.

The later poems fall naturally into certain groups. Among other groupings, some of the poems deal with Christmas, some with Easter, and some, like the one I am about to read, relate to both holidays. This is "The Resurrection and the Life," Helen's penultimate poem. It is unusual in the sense that it is really two poems in one. In its entirety the poem consists of seven stanzas that share the same complicated rhyme scheme, wherein each stanza has six lines, with the second, fourth, and sixth lines in rhyme. There is thus a unity of *form*, but the *content* differs between the first four stanzas and the last three. Helen actually insisted that they were two separate poems, and when she had finished her original typing for us to go over, she drew a line between the fourth and fifth stanzas. For some reason, however, it was printed as one poem.

---

6. *The Gifts of God*, p. 100.

We are going to read only the first four stanzas here, because they stand alone and are somewhat separate in content from the last three. In many ways this poem unifies much of what I have spoken about so far: what it means to be loving, and silent to the ego.

> You think Him dead Who rose again for you,
> And so you cannot see the shining light
> In which you are delivered. Come, My child,
> And judge Him not. He is not dead. So bright
> His radiance that nothing still remains
> Obscured from Heaven in the doubt of night.

While this clearly is a reference to Jesus, in terms of the poem's meaning it really refers to the Son of God we think has been crucified. We are taken in by appearances, and so the poem begins: "You think Him dead Who rose again for you, / And so you cannot see the shining light / In which you are delivered."

All we see is the ego's darkness, and not the light it has covered over. Earlier in this book I explained how the ego tries to put a solid wall of granite between ourselves and the light, but when we begin the process of forgiveness we get closer to this wall of sin and death, realizing it is nothing. What appeared before to be so solid is now nothing but a flimsy veil, through which, with Jesus beside us, we see the light. Even though our guilt feels like a heavy and impenetrable block, we come to realize it is not solid at all, being nothing more or less than a silly thought. Yet this wisp of an illusion has given rise to a world of sacrifice, suffering, and death (i.e., crucifixion). And so the poem tells us we should not judge against the Son of God, because He is not dead: "So bright His radiance that nothing still / Remains obscured from Heaven in the doubt of night" means that the light is still there. Not one light in Heaven's firmament has ceased to shine. We continue:

> So still the birth you did not understand
> Who came to you. Before your frightened eyes
> The Lord of light and life appears to fail
> His promises of Heaven's grace, and dies
> Forever on a cross. Nor can you see
> The Child of hope Who in a manger lies.

The specific reference, again, is to Jesus; this time his birth and death. But in a larger sense this is a portrait of the Son of God in all of us. Being a Child of God, Love, and Heaven's grace, we should have lived eternally. Yet the ego's dream tells us that was a lie; so we do not see the hope for all the darkness of death. We see only the body: its seeming birth and seeming death. Life in the world *is* a crucifixion, ending inevitably in death, and we forget all this is a sham, a flimsy veil drawn across reality. It is a dream, yet within its veils of deception it appears so compellingly real we forget what we secretly know to be true, and cannot see "The Child of hope Who in a manger lies."

Regardless of what goes on in the world, we all have a right mind: the Word of the Atonement that calls us to us through the loving presence of the Holy Spirit. There always remains the Child Who awaits our turning back to Him, despite our being taken in by appearances. In this regard I always like to mention Plato, who, twenty-five hundred years ago, taught the difference between appearance and reality. His famous Allegory of the Cave depicts the distinction between the shadows seen on the interior wall of a cave, and the sun's light that casts the shadows. The material world witnesses to our total confusion, for all we see are the shadows of appearance. These shadows are pretty terrible, for they keep the light hidden behind their veils of forgetfulness. We forget the illuminating star of Christmas—the birth of Christ shining in each of us—for we perversely choose not to see it. Our next stanza:

> The wise are silent. Stand you by a while
> And let the wise men show you what they see
> That came of you from stillness and from peace
> Which rest in you, but speak to them of Me.
> And then be comforted. The living Lord
> Has come again where He has willed to be.

This is a specific reference to the mythic wise men who attended the birth of Jesus, but the "wise" here have nothing to do with the magi ("magicians") of biblical lore. Here, they represent the "advanced teachers of God" (M-4.2:2) who know the difference between appearance and reality. They know what it means to love and be silent midst the ego's darkness, the battleground on which blood is forever spilled—the world of specialness, hate, murder, deception, and pain. Standing tall, they smile sweetly and say, "This is nothing." They truly know the ego's darkness requires no response, correction, or healing, because there is nothing to respond *to*. These are "the wise," and that is why they are silent.

Some of you may remember Helen's image of Michelangelo's wonderful Pieta, where Mary is holding the crumpled body of her dead son. Seeing this in her mind, Helen heard Mary say, "This means nothing." Such a response exemplifies the "wise," who can look upon one of our greatest symbols of the world's reality—the gruesomely painful and unjustified death of an innocent and loving man—and can say: "This means nothing."

"The wise are silent" because there is nothing to say. We saw earlier how Cordelia stood before her father who was in the throes of a massive ego attack, and thinks to herself: "*What is Cordelia to say?...* *Love, and be silent.*" That is all that loving wisdom does in the face of madness. No matter how hideous and vicious its form, the advanced teachers of God simply stand before it, quietly love and say nothing, meaning of course nothing from the ego. There is no need to respond—in thought, not behavior—because response makes it real. That is why "the wise" are silent. Thus: "Stand you by a while / And let the wise men show you what they see." Let us be taught by these wise men; and let us be taught by that Wise Man within us, Who wants only to teach us what He knows, and share with us the love that comes from a wisdom not of this world.

They come "of you from stillness and from peace," which rest *in* you, not outside. These wise men represent our right-minded thought, the Holy Spirit, Who cannot be separate from us as He *is* us, but not the "us" we think we are. He is the memory of Who we are—the Thought of Christ that is our Self—that we took with us into our sleep of separation, when the dream began. And all the while we sleep, this Memory remains in our minds as the lovely reminder that what we think we see is false, being simply appearance and not reality, only a flimsy veil that stands between us and the truth.

These wise men speak about Jesus as he says, "but speak to them of Me. / And then be comforted." Jesus is a wonderful symbol that demonstrates the difference between appearance and reality. His birth was an illusion, as was his death. But his love was not. The form, which people idolize, was nothing:

> The man was an illusion, for he seemed to be a separate being, walking by himself, within a body that appeared to hold his self from Self, as all illusions do.... His little life on earth was not enough to teach the mighty lesson that he learned for all of you. He will remain with you to lead you from the hell you made to God (C-5.2:3; 5:3-4).

It is the love he represents that is everything; not a love that is his as a person, but what abides in the *mind* of God's one Son, of which we are an indivisible part. When you allow yourself to be in the presence of that love, you realize there is nothing going on here, nothing that requires a response. You simply love, as your gentle smile says: "What I see means nothing."

"The living Lord / Has come again where He has willed to be" refers to the rebirth of the Child: "Christ is reborn as but a little Child each time a wanderer would leave his home" (W-pI.182.10:1). It means He has always been within us, so it is not that He has really come again. There can be no Second Coming of Jesus, for he knows he never left. In Chapter 4 of the text Jesus speaks of the First Coming of Christ as the creation (T-4.IV.10). Then seems to come the interim period when we fell asleep. The Second Coming is when we, as God's one Son, awaken from the dream of separation: "The Second Coming of Christ means nothing more than the end of the ego's rule and the healing of the mind" (T-4.IV.10:2).

The Second Coming thus has nothing to do with Jesus, nor with Christ or God. *We* are the ones who fell asleep; therefore we are the ones who awaken, and that is the Second Coming. It is really not the living Lord who has come again; it is we who have come to our senses and return to the living Lord we never left. Now, the final stanza we will read:

> Wait now for morning. In the silence hear
> The winged whispering that hails the Son
> In quiet certainty and lovely calm
> Whom death released to life. He is the One
> For Whom you wait. Then look again on Him,
> And join His benediction, "It is done."

The phrase "Wait now for morning" suggests patience. I mentioned earlier that one of the characteristics of the advanced teacher of God is that he is patient because he is certain of the outcome. So what is the hurry? He knows the morning has come and salvation already accomplished; forgiveness is done and the world already over (T-28.I.1:6). There is no reason for the impatience that says something has to be done right away. Any time you think you receive a message from Jesus urging you to do something—time is running out, better get with the program—you know its source is not him. No pressure ever comes from his infinite gentleness and patience. There is simply that loving and silent reminder of love, which by its very presence calls in the quiet voice that says: "Come back home." That presence knows we are already home, so there is no urgency or pressure of time.

We "wait now for morning" because that is when the sun rises: both sun and Son in his rebirth. In time it has not yet happened, because there remains a part of us that is confused about appearance and reality, but we have let the wise men in and will listen to their gentle counsel. That is why we wait in certainty and silence, in which we hear the lovely phrase: "The winged whispering that hails the Son / In quiet certainty and lovely calm." The Holy Spirit is our "winged whisperer." His Voice is quietly soft. He need not raise It because He knows there is nothing to shout over. Our loudness comes only when we insist on being heard. Love never shouts because it knows the nothingness of the ego's raucous shrieks. It does not even hear it. Thus we are told in the text:

> The Voice of the Holy Spirit does not command, because It is in-capable of arrogance. It does not demand, because It does not seek control. It does not overcome, because It does not attack. It merely reminds. It is compelling only because of what It reminds you *of*. It brings to your mind the other way, remaining quiet even in the midst of the turmoil you may make. The Voice for God is always quiet, because It speaks of peace (T-5.II.7:1-7).

Our lives should be as close as possible to that ideal of loving silence. As much we can, we strive to identify with the patient, loving, and silent presence of the "winged whispering," especially when tempted to lose our peace. Becoming upset is not difficult in our world, for temptations abound. However, the still, small voice of the Holy Spirit is our constant Answer. The point is to see "love, and be silent" as an ideal, not something to force, and then crucify ourselves for fail-ing to live up to. It is an ideal towards which we grow. Let these inner wise men gently guide us to the place we never left, the home we never betrayed. They represent the "quiet certainty and lovely calm / Whom death released to life." That is the meaning of being reborn from the ego's life, which is death. We are born again by having a second chance to choose the Holy Spirit instead of the ego. Once we have cho-sen correctly, we look on the risen Christ and remember the resurrection: *our* awakening from the dream of death.

Resurrection is another area in which the Churches misunderstood Jesus' message. By focusing on what eyes could see, as if there were something tangible to behold, as if rising in a body were meaningful, the early Christians missed the point of changing one's *mind*. There could certainly have been an experience some had, symbolizing the inner awakening in physical form because they thought they were bodies. But it was not an awakening that really happened in the physical figure of Jesus, but an awakening in each of us to which he was pointing. By continuing to see it only in him, we exclude ourselves and see resurrection as something *he* did, because he was different and special: *the* Son of God, who thus could do things we could not. Yet his message was that the resurrection is something he did for all of us, by showing us it *could* be done. That is why he says in the clarification of terms, speaking of himself in the third person:

> He [Jesus] offers thanks to you as well as him for you arose with him when he began to save the world. And you will be with him when time is over and no trace remains of dreams of spite in which you dance to death's thin melody (C-6.5:5-6).

When Jesus awoke, we all awoke because God's Son is one. Resurrection is not what happened in one man, during a certain period of history. It happened in the *mind* of God's one Son, outside time and space. Listening to the "wise men" and hearing "the winged whispering" of their loving silence, we "Then look again on Him, / And join His benediction, 'It is done.'" That is the acceptance of the Atonement and the happy end of the ego's dream of crucifixion.

CLOSING MEDITATION

"The Holy Christ Is Born in Me Today"

Turn now to the workbook and we will close with Lesson 303. "The holy Christ is born in me today" was written around Christmas, and is a beautiful, beautiful lesson. Because of the season in which it was written, Christmas imagery runs through it, but obviously it is not about the birth of Jesus, for it reflects the rebirth of Christ in all of us. Thus the lesson nicely knits together the themes we have been discussing, including our silence to the sounds of the ego. We read, for example, this line: "Let earthly sounds be quiet." When we actively choose against them, we let the earthly sounds be quiet so that we hear love's "winged whispering." That is how we "let Him hear the sounds He understands": the soundless song, the silent melody of love that is always there to greet our return, at the same time it makes such return a reality.

The holy Christ is born in me today.

Watch with me, angels, watch with me today. Let all God's holy Thoughts surround me, and be still with me while Heaven's Son is born. Let earthly sounds be quiet, and the sights to which I am accustomed disappear. Let Christ be welcomed where He is at home. And let Him hear the sounds He understands, and see but sights that show His Father's Love. Let Him no longer be a stranger here, for He is born again in me today.

Your Son is welcome, Father. He has come to save me from the evil self I made. He is the Self that You have given me. He is but what I really am in truth. He is the Son You love above all things. He is my Self as You created me. It is not Christ that can be crucified. Safe in Your Arms let me receive Your Son.

INDEX OF REFERENCES TO *A COURSE IN MIRACLES*

text

T-in.1:6-7	85	T-19.IV-A.i	62
T-1.II.3:5-4:1	79	T-19.IV-A.17:1-2	65
T-2.III.3:10	56	T-19.IV-B.8:1	65
T-2.V.18	40	T-20	61
T-2.VI.4:3	66	T-20.IV.4:7	63
T-2.VII.1:4-6	72	T-21.I	49
T-3.VI.3:1	51	T-21.VII.7:8	92
T-4.I.1:1-3; 5:1-2	82	T-23.II.6	40
T-4.III.8:2	91	T-23.II.11	16
T-4.IV.10	99	T-23.IV	50
T-4.IV.10:2	99	T-23.IV.9:8	71
T-4.VI.4	70	T-24.II.4:3-5:1	19
T-4.VI.8:2	95	T-24.V.4	74
T-4.VII.3:6	87	T-25.VI	58
T-4.VII.8	40	T-25.VII.5	74
T-5.II.7:1-7	100	T-26.V.13:1	29
T-5.VI.3:5	4	T-26.IX.4:1	57
T-6.I	33	T-27.I	33
T-6.V-C	43	T-27.I.4:6	45
T-7.VIII.3:9-12	69	T-27.III	88
T-10.I.2:1	22	T-27.VIII.7:2-5; 8:1	69-70
T-10.III.10:1-2	87	T-27.VIII.8	59
T-13.in.2:2-10	5	T-27.VIII.10:1	86
T-13.III.10	14	T-28.I.1:6	99
T-15	61	T-28.II	33
T-15.IV.9:1-2	91	T-28.IV	82
T-15.VIII	89	T-28.VI.1:1	50
T-15.XI	67-92	T-29.IV.2:2-6	21
T-16	70	T-29.VII	86
T-16.V	90	T-31	78
T-16.V.10:1	54	T-31.V.2:6	17
T-18.VI.1:5-6	87	T-31.V.5:3	34
T-18.VII	36	T-31.VIII.2:3	53
T-18.VII.3:1	67	T-31.VIII.9:2	65
T-18.VII.8	36	T-31.VIII.12:5	78
T-19	61		

workbook for students

W-pI.49.4:3 19

W-pI.106.2:1 49

W.pI.133 46

W-pI.137 77

W-pI.155.1:2-3 52

W-pI.161.7:1 50

W-pI.169.5:4 30

W-pI.170.8:7 20

W-pI.182 .... 27, 41, 73, 74

W-pI.182.2:1 28

W-pI.182.4 39-60

W-pI.182.10:1 99

W-pI.187.10:2-3 87

W-pII.1 82

W-pII.1.4:1 30

W-pII.226 50

W-pII.226.2 50

W-pII.3.2:1 84

W-pII.4.5:2 50

W-pII.253 59

W-pII.303 103

manual for teachers

M-in.2:1 82

M-4.2:2 97

M-13.1:2 50

M-17.7:4 30

M-17.7:11 75

M-21.1:9-10 88

M-23.4:1-2 79

clarification of terms

C-5.2:3; 5:3-4 98

C-5.5:7 80

C-6.5:1 81

C-6.5:5-6 101

Psychotherapy: Purpose, Process and Practice

P-2.IV.1:7 .... 59, 84

P-3.III.8:12-13 83

The Song of Prayer

S-1.in.1:2-4 88

S-2.II 34

The Gifts of God

"The Ancient Love" (p. 44) 25-26, 34, 43, 46

"Conversion" (p. 61) 27-36

"The Holiness of Christmas" (p. 97) 23-25

"The Resurrection and the Life" (p. 100) 95-101

"The Soundless Song" (p. 76) 22